THE ENCYCLOPEDIA
OF SANDWICHES

THE ENCYCLOPEDIA OF SANDWICHES

RECIPES, HISTORY, AND TRIVIA
FOR EVERYTHING BETWEEN SLICED BREAD

by Susan Russo
photography by Matt Armendariz

QUIRK BOOKS
PHILADELPHIA

Copyright © 2010 by Quirk Productions, Inc.

Library of Congress Cataloging in Publication Number: 2010933869

ISBN: 978-1-59474-438-9

Printed in China

Typeset in Berthold Akzidenz Grotesk and Bell MT

Designed by Jenny Kraemer
Production management by John J. McGurk
Photography by Matt Armendariz
Editorial assistance by Jane Morley and Alexandra Bitzer

Quirk Books
215 Church Street
Philadelphia, PA 19106
www.quirkbooks.com

10 9 8 7 6 5 4 3 2 1

FOR MY DAD, who has proudly told every single person in Rhode Island about this book.

FOR MY MOM, who has happily tested every recipe in this book.

FOR MY HUSBAND, who has eaten every sandwich in this book. Often more than once.

ENJOY EVERY SANDWICH.

—Warren Zevon

TABLE OF CONTENTS

Acknowledgments

Thanks to sandwich lovers everywhere.

Special thanks to Margaret McGuire, my editor. She's smart, funny, creative, and patient, everything an editor should be. Many thanks to Matt Armendariz and Jenny Kraemer for making humble sandwiches look glamorous; the Quirk staff who helped make this book a reality; sandwich aficionados Jane Morley and Alexandra Bitzer for their research and editorial support; the readers of my website, Food Blogga, for their encouragement; Brad Walker of the Brown Hotel in Louisville, Kentucky, for sharing the hotel's iconic Hot Brown sandwich; the "Three Guys From Miami," Glenn Lindgren, Raul Musibay, and Jorge Castillo, for sharing their recipe for the Cuban Sandwich, first printed in their cookbook *Three Guys From Miami Cook Cuban*; Terry Thompson-Anderson, author of *Cajun-Creole Cooking*, and Kathy Shearer of Shearer Publishing, Fredericksburg, Texas, for allowing me to reprint Ms. Thompson-Anderson's recipe for the New Orleans oyster loaf; Steve Lupo of Lupo's Spiedies in Binghampton, New York, for teaching me about the spiedie's history and for sharing tips on making them at home; the folks at Campanile Restaurant in Los Angeles—in particular, Mark Peel, the executive chef—for sharing the recipe for an open-faced burrata sandwich; Jesse Goldstein, owner of Nashville's famous Loveless Café, for sharing their recipe for chicken salad; the Primanti Brothers for sharing their recipe for a homemade version of the classic Primanti; Jane Bitto of Evelyn's Diner in Tiverton, Rhode Island, for sharing her recipe for the singular Chow Mein Sandwich; John Brunetto of Mona Lisa Italian Foods in San Diego for his tips on making a memorable Caprese sandwich; the good people at Venda Ravioli in Providence, Rhode Island, for sharing their recipe for Bresaola and Arugula Sandwich, and to Chris Spertini, in particular, for his time. And thanks to my recipe testers Zaira Avolos, Eilenn Anonical, Deborah Balint, Jayne Belz, Carrie Boyd, Sarah Caron, Susannah Chen, Mike DiEva, Leslie Frasier, Annie Gallo, Valerie Harrison, Elly Kafritsas, Michael Kindness, Laetitia Laure, Lisa Lawless, Deb Mahon, Hilary Marsfelder, Amy Morgan, Rachel Narins, Karen Padilla, Stacey Rittenberg, Kate Selner, Mike Stephens, Brianne Smith, and Kasia Wolny.

Thanks to my mom for always saying, "Sure, honey, anything for you," every time I asked her to test a recipe. Thanks to my dad for being my most loyal fan. And thanks to my husband, Jeff, for eating more sandwiches in the course of a few months than he had in his entire lifetime. And for not complaining when his jeans got tight. I would have.

Introduction

A Tribute to the Greatest Invention since Sliced Bread

Hello, Sandwich Lovers!

Have you eaten a sandwich today? Odds are you have. Hundreds of *millions* of people across the globe do every single day.

It's not surprising. The simple combination of bread and filling is a remarkable culinary invention: it's satisfying, fast, comforting, and portable. Not only do we love to eat sandwiches, but we also love to make them, talk about them, and gaze upon them. Entire books, television shows, and websites have been devoted to this modest food. Some people have traveled the world eating nothing but sandwiches. Others write poems about them.

Why are we so passionate? Because sandwiches typically have deep cultural, ethnic, and geographic roots. Think of the Vietnamese bahn mi, the Italian panino, and the American fluffernutter; each has its own delicious story, and we cherish those stories almost as much as the sandwiches themselves.

Sandwiches are among the most democratic of foods. They're perfect day or night. They can be a quick snack or a bona fide meal. Decadent or plain, six inches or six feet, sandwiches have always been honest, filling food. They're affordable yet nutritious. They can be eaten just about anywhere, including over the kitchen sink. And they're gloriously unfussy.

Yet sandwich purists (yes, they exist, and if you're reading this, you're likely one of them), will argue that a sandwich isn't "just a sandwich." It can be humble or high-brow. In the right hands, it can be a culinary pièce de résistance.

What Makes a Sandwich a **Sandwich**?
The Great Sandwich Debate

This hands-on staple has evolved from its humble beginnings to include a series of delicious and exclusive anomalies. Originally, a sandwich was any of a variety of fillings held together with two or more slices of bread. After years of tasty experimentation, the fillings now range from meat and cheese to French fries and spaghetti. And don't *even* get started on bread—rolls and buns, sure, but what about waffles, biscuits, cakes, and cookies?

People are just as passionate about what can or cannot be a sandwich as they are about how to build one. In fact, the debate became so heated that, in 2006, it went to court in a food-chain lawsuit between Panera Bread Co. and Qdoba Mexican Grill. In the case, a Massachusetts court set the unfortunate precedent that burritos, quesadillas, wraps, and tacos are not legally part of our beloved sandwich family. Perhaps, in the years to come, these less-bready cousins will be legally allowed to join the venerated rank of sandwiches. But, for the purposes of this *Encyclopedia of Sandwiches*, a sandwich is defined as a variety of fillings snuggled lovingly between two sides or slices of leavened eatables—unless, of course, it is open-faced, in which case only one leavened surface is required. Yes, dear reader, this definition includes the likes of the **Hamburger** and the **Hot Dog**, thanks to their basic construction and historical categorization. And you'll see such iconic sandwiches as the **Classic Club**, the **Reuben**, and the **Sloppy Joe** sharing space with forgotten gems like the **Sandwich Loaf** and quirky up-and-comers like the **Muffinwich** and the **Banana Split Sandwich**.

The Evolution of the Sandwich
From the Earl of Sandwich to Colonel Sanders

Our beloved snack has inauspicious roots. In 1762 in England, the fourth Earl of Sandwich, an inveterate gambler, demanded a handheld meal of meat placed between two slices of bread so that he wouldn't have to leave the gaming table for his repast. As Alan Davidson notes, the earl may not have been the first person to place food between two slices of bread, but he is responsible for igniting a "culinary revolution that has gained momentum ever since."

Although the English introduced sandwiches to America, they didn't become a staple of cuisine there until 1837, when Eliza Leslie included a recipe for a ham sandwich in her book *Miss Leslie's Direction for Cookery*. Along with ham, popular fillings for these earliest creations were sardines, tongue, cheese, nuts, and fruit jellies.

The late nineteenth and early twentieth centuries ushered in an array of hefty, ethnic sandwiches courtesy of immigrant communities, notably, the **Hero**, the **Muffaletta**, and **Pastrami on Rye**.

In 1930 the introduction of packaged sliced Wonder bread revolutionized the sandwich, helping harried cooks quickly turn out lunch-counter favorites like the **BLT** to hungry customers. A decade later, moms were sending their little soldiers to school clutching that World War II–era classic, the **PB&J**. The 1940s, '50s, and '60s saw an increase in lunch box, picnic, and "lady's luncheon" treats such as **Bologna**, **Meatloaf**, and **Peanut Butter** sandwiches as well as the consummate **Chicken**, **Egg**, and **Tuna Salad** sandwiches. The prominence of breakfast sandwiches, as well as the **Roast Beef** and **Chicken** sandwiches, came about in the 1970s, thanks to the explosion of fast-food chains. And in the last three decades, gourmet sandwiches have made their mark.

Sandwiches are constantly evolving. New takes on old favorites as well as entirely novel creations are always cropping up. Artisanal versions of the **Chicken Sandwich** and the **Grilled Cheese** have helped elevate the sandwich's modest status, and retro basics are making a comeback, often with a modern twist. Hip eateries are serving comforting, homey sandwiches such as **Chicken-Fried Steak** and hot open-face **Turkey** sandwiches smothered with brown gravy. And fast-food chains are dreaming up supersize versions like Hardee's calorie-busting Monster Thickburger or the KFC Double Down Chicken Sandwich, cheese and bacon gathered not between bread but between two fried chicken patties.

Decadent or plain, extravagant or simple, sandwiches have always been good, filling food for working men and women. Everyone loves them. In fact, there's evidence that sandwiches have been one of humanity's favorite foods since biblical times. In fact, Passover has long been celebrated with what may have been the first sandwich recipe: lamb, eaten together with unleavened bread and bitter herbs. It's nothing fancy—just a simple, delicious meal between bread.

Ingredient Index

A sandwich for every imaginable ingredient

"I've got brown sandwiches or green sandwiches—it's either very new cheese or very old meat."
—Oscar Madison in *The Odd Couple* by Neil Simon

Ingredients are important. If you want more choices than just brown sandwiches or green sandwiches, this index will help. Even if you have only a few odd ingredients in your fridge, chances are you can make a delicious meal out of them.

THE ENCYCLOPEDIA
OF SANDWICHES A–Z

All-in-One Breakfast Sandwich
A serious knife-and-fork affair

The iconic breakfast sandwich is the simple bacon, egg, and cheese or Egg McMuffin, a fast-food version of eggs Benedict dreamed up and dropped into a to-go sack by inventive McDonald's franchisee Herb Peterson in 1972. But today a whole new class of over-the-top breakfast sandwiches—made with pancakes, French toast, or waffles—is popping up on the menus of fast-food chains, coffee shops, and food trucks. Of course, you don't have to go out to enjoy them; whether you serve them at brunch or as "breakfast for dinner," they're the ideal way to use up leftovers.

About 2 tablespoons butter
2 cooked waffles
2 eggs cooked to your liking
2 strips cooked bacon
½ cooked hash brown patty
Maple syrup, to taste

❶ Butter both sides of waffles. On a griddle over medium-high heat, cook 1 minute, or until golden and hot. Remove from heat. Add eggs, bacon, and hash browns.

❷ Drizzle with maple syrup and close sandwich. Makes 1

Mix 'n' Match!

Bread
Pancakes
Waffles
French toast

Fillings
Chicken-fried steak with gravy
Steak and eggs
Baked apples or pears with maple syrup
   and nuts
Peanut butter and jelly
Bananas and honey
Cream cheese with strawberries

Artisanal Grilled Cheese
Gooey deluxe grilled sandwiches

The humble **Grilled Cheese** sandwich remained relatively unchanged for decades, until creative chefs began taking a new look at the old classic. In the late 1990s, Nancy Silverton inaugurated Thursday Grilled Cheese Night at her Los Angeles restaurant Campanile. Offering high-priced, high-style versions such as Gorgonzola with roasted radicchio, walnuts, and honey, Silverton quickly ushered in a whole new world of designer sandwiches. Artisanal Grilled Cheese sandwiches incorporate handcrafted breads, such as kalamata olive or rosemary and olive oil, and gourmet cheeses, such as Gruyère or burrata. In addition, they're often topped with sweet and savory fillings, everything from caramelized onions to apricot marmalade. This recipe is courtesy of executive chef Mark Peel of Campanile.

---

3 to 4 garlic cloves, sliced, plus 2 whole garlic cloves for rubbing bread

1½ tablespoons olive oil, plus more for drizzling

8 ounces cherry tomatoes

Salt and freshly ground black pepper, to taste

4 slices sourdough bread

1 pound burrata cheese, cut into ¼-inch slices

4 ounces (½ cup) chickpeas

Salsa Verde (see opposite)

4 slices prosciutto

❶ Preheat oven to 500°F. In a skillet, add garlic and 1 cup cold water; cover and bring to a boil over medium heat. Drain garlic and return to pan; 1 cup cold water, cover, and bring to a boil again; remove from heat. Drain water and pat garlic dry. In the same pan, heat oil over medium heat and fry 1 to 2 minutes, being careful not to burn it.

❷ Spread cherry tomatoes on a baking sheet. Drizzle with a little olive oil, salt, and pepper and roast 10 minutes. Remove from oven and let cool. Toss with chickpeas and salsa verde.

❸ Grill or toast bread slices. Transfer to a serving plate and rub with garlic. Place 2 to 3 cheese slices on each bread slice. Top each with one-quarter of the tomato-chickpea mixture and 1 slice prosciutto. Sprinkle with fried garlic chips. Makes 4 open-faced sandwiches

Salsa Verde

Though typically associated with Mexican cuisine, this green sauce has a decidedly Mediterranean flavor profile thanks to the addition of anchovies, capers, and garlic.

3 or 4 (3-inch) salt-packed anchovies, rinsed well, backbone removed, and finely chopped (about 1 tablespoon)

2 tablespoons plus ½ teaspoon capers, rinsed and finely chopped

3 garlic cloves, peeled and finely chopped

½ teaspoon kosher salt, plus more to taste

½ cup plus 2 tablespoons chopped fresh flat-leaf parsley

1 tablespoon plus 1½ teaspoons coarsely chopped fresh marjoram leaves

1 tablespoon plus 1½ teaspoons coarsely chopped fresh mint leaves

¾ cup extra-virgin olive oil

Fresh lemon juice, to taste

❶ Using a mortar and pestle, pulverize anchovies, capers, garlic, and salt to a smooth paste. (If you don't have a mortar and pestle, thinly chop ingredients and smash with the flat of a knife; you can also use a small food processor to puree them.)

❷ Add parsley, marjoram, and mint and continue pulverizing to break down herbs. Slowly add olive oil, stirring well to combine. Just before serving, season to taste with salt and lemon juice. Makes about 1 cup

5

A
B

Sweet and Savory Variations

- Grilled Brie, sliced pears, and honey mustard on French bread.
- Grilled Gruyère, caramelized onions, and sage on sourdough bread.
- Grilled buffalo mozzarella, olive tapenade, and fresh basil on ciabatta bread.
- Grilled buffalo mozzarella, prosciutto, and pesto on sundried tomato bread.
- Grilled Jarlsberg and Granny Smith apple on raisin bread.

"I went into a French restaurant and asked the waiter,
'Have you got frog's legs?' He said, 'Yes,' so I said,
'Well, hop into the kitchen and get me a cheese sandwich.'"
—Tommy Cooper

A
B

Bagel and Lox
A New York City classic

Most culinary historians agree that the modern-day bagel originated in Jewish communities in Poland in the early seventeenth century. Eastern European Jewish immigrants introduced both bagels and Bagels and Lox to America at the turn of the twentieth century. By the 1950s, the bagel was a mainstream American food. Though bagels and lox were traditionally found only in New York's Jewish delis, today they're widely available, especially at chains such as Bruegger's and Einstein Bros. Of course, not all bagels and lox are created equal, so if you're a stickler for authenticity, reserve your patronage for the New York Jewish delis or eateries.

A truly great Bagel and Lox combination relies on the highest quality ingredients: a fresh bagel split in half and topped with an ample spread of smooth cream cheese and silky cured salmon. Favored garnishes include capers and thinly sliced red onions; dill and chive cream cheeses are popular alternatives to plain. If you don't have a Jewish market or deli nearby, purchase a freshly baked plain or poppy seed bagel (no rubbery day-old bagels allowed), rich cream cheese whipped to a pillow-soft consistency, and thinly sliced cured salmon that is soft and pink.

---

1 cup cream cheese, preferably whipped

3 tablespoons fresh chives, finely chopped

3 tablespoons fresh dill, finely chopped

Salt and freshly ground black pepper, to taste

2 large plain or poppy seed bagels, halved
   lengthwise

8 ounces cured smoked salmon

1 sprig dill, broken into fronds, for garnish

❶ In a small bowl, mix together cream cheese, chives, dill, salt, and pepper. Spread mixture evenly across 4 bagel halves.

❷ Top each with 2 ounces salmon. Garnish with dill. Serve immediately. Makes 4

Try mixing a few coarsly chopped capers
into the cream cheese mixture.

Baked Bean Sandwich

Humble New England fare

A long-standing Saturday night meal in Massachusetts, the Baked Bean Sandwich consists of two slices of thick, chewy brown bread that is buttered and topped with Boston baked beans, a singular sweet bean mixture traditionally made with molasses and brown sugar.

Though the earliest known recipe for a baked bean sandwich was published in 1909, its origins can be traced to colonial Massachusetts: Pilgrims, who did not believe in cooking on Sundays, prepared large batches of baked beans and loaves of brown bread on Saturdays. The humble baked bean sandwich—which reflects traditional Yankee values, such as practicality, unpretentiousness, and thriftiness—has withstood the test of time and continues to be enjoyed by many New Englanders.

Brown bread is so named because of its characteristically dark color, which it derives from molasses. You can substitute toasted pumpernickel or whole wheat. For a less messy affair, lightly mash the beans with a fork to create a thicker paste. Otherwise, be sure to have some extra bread handy to sop up the sticky, sweet sauce that's sure to drip onto your plate.

About 1 tablespoon butter
2 thick slices brown bread
¼ cup baked beans, preferably Boston-style
  with molasses, heated

Butter both slices of bread. Pour warm baked beans onto bread, buttered side up. Makes 1

Since 1927, Heinz has promoted open-faced Beans on Toast as a way to serve tasty baked beans for breakfast as well as dinner.

A
B

Beans, Beans . . .

- Piccalilli Baked Bean Sandwiches: Mix ¼ cup baked beans with 1 tablespoon applesauce and 2 teaspoons piccalilli. Spoon over the bread and top with 2 slices baked ham and 2 slices Jarlsberg or cheddar cheese. To serve hot, butter the bread and toast it; quickly top each piece with a slice of cheese so it will melt. Panfry the ham until crisp and place on top of the cheese. Add a scoop of the bean-and-relish mixture, close the sandwich, and serve immediately.

- Italian Beans on Toast: Make this variation with thick slices of leftover Italian bread moistened with water; drizzle with extra-virgin olive oil and toast lightly. Top with drained cannellini beans seasoned with extra-virgin olive oil salt, crushed red pepper flakes, grated Parmesan cheese, and herbs such as basil and parsley. Serve hot and open-faced.

Baked bean sandwiches are often served with a traditional relish or piccalilli, a savory relish made of pickled vegetables and spices.

Banana Bread Sandwich

A toasty sweet treat

Two hunks of fresh or toasty grilled banana bread can be sandwiched with sweet ingredients, such as ice cream, grilled bananas, or peanut butter and jelly. Banana bread is a quick bread—a sweet, cakey type made with baking soda instead of yeast—that contains mashed ripe bananas. It is typically flavored with vanilla extract, cinnamon, and chopped nuts. Making banana bread from scratch is easy, but for a truly low-maintenance brunch, a store-bought loaf is your best bet. Thanks to well-known chefs such as Paula Deen, this old-fashioned favorite has been getting a lot of attention as the foundation of a delicious dessert sandwich.

VANILLA SPICE CREAM CHEESE
1 (8-ounce) package cream cheese
¼ teaspoon ground cinnamon
⅛ teaspoon pure vanilla extract
2 tablespoons pure maple syrup
¼ teaspoon pure maple extract

1 loaf banana bread, thinly sliced
3 tablespoons butter, divided
2 ripe bananas, sliced on the diagonal

❶ In a bowl with a mixer, combine cream cheese and cinnamon. Slowly add vanilla, maple syrup, and maple extract, beating until smooth and fluffy.

❷ Butter both sides of banana bread slices. Place on a hot griddle and toast 2 minutes per side; set aside. In the same griddle, melt butter, add banana slices, and cook 1 minute per side, or until golden. Sandwich cream cheese mixture and grilled bananas and serve warm. Makes 4 to 6

Go Bananas!

- Banana Bread Tea Sandwiches: Cut sandwiches into finger-length pieces.
- Banana Bread PB&Js: Use banana bread instead of white bread.
- Banana Bread Elvis: Smother sliced bananas and bacon with peanut butter on grilled banana bread.
- Banana Bread Ice Cream Sandwiches: Place a scoop or two of ice cream between two slices of grilled banana bread.

Banana Bread Sandwich

Banana Split Sandwich

All this deluxe snack needs is a tall glass of cold milk

In the 1920s one of the most popular soda fountain treats was a banana split, made with scoops of chocolate, strawberry, and vanilla ice cream nestled between a split banana and topped with hot fudge, strawberry and pineapple sauces, along with a generous heap of whipped cream. The whole delicacy was garnished with nuts and maraschino cherries.

No one person is credited with inventing the Banana Split Sandwich, but it's my guess that one day an imaginative mother concocted it to satisfy a fussy child. No matter who dreamed it up, this sandwich is an easy way to delight children—and a sure way to make any adult feel like a kid again.

About 2 tablespoons butter

2 thick slices white bread, such as country white or Texas toast

1 tablespoon creamy or chunky peanut butter

1 to 2 teaspoons chocolate sauce or hot fudge

1 small banana, cut lengthwise, then in halves (4 pieces total)

1 tablespoon strawberry jam

1 tablespoon pineapple jam

❶ Butter 1 side of each bread slice; place buttered side down.

❷ Spread peanut butter and chocolate sauce one 1 slice, and top with 2 banana pieces. Spread jams on the other, and top with remaining banana pieces. Close sandwich.

❸ Place on a griddle over medium-high heat. Cook 1 to 2 minutes, flip gently, and cook 1 minute more, or until bread is golden and toasty. Makes 1

Tasty Toppings

- Substitute Nutella or mini chocolate chips for the chocolate sauce.

- Try sliced fresh strawberries and pineapple instead of jam, and add marshmallow crème, crushed nuts, or caramel sauce.

Bánh Mì

A delicious and healthy Vietnamese hoagie

This Vietnamese sandwich is made of a crunchy, toasted baguette filled with pickled carrots and daikon, julienned vegetables, fresh cilantro, spicy pâté, hot chili sauce, special Vietnamese mayonnaise, and your choice of meat, seafood, or tofu.

Pronounced "BUN-mee," the Bánh Mì may be the greatest fusion sandwich. It originated in Vietnam during French occupation. French colonists introduced the Vietnamese to sandwiches, which they made with wheat baguettes filled with pâté, meats, and vegetables. The Vietnamese soon made their own baguettes with rice flour, creating the uniquely crusty-on-the-outside, airy-on-the-inside quality for which they are famous. Common fillings included pâté, meats such as pork roll (a Vietnamese bologna), julienned vegetables, fresh herbs, mayonnaise, and hot chilis. Bánh Mì were introduced to North America by Vietnamese immigrants in the wake of the Vietnam War. Though originally found only in places like New York's Chinatown, Bánh Mì are now served across North America and parts of Europe as well; local variations are known as "Tofu hoagies," "Vietnamese hoagies," "Vietnamese subs," or "Vietnamese po'boys." These tasty, affordable sandwiches are a healthy alternative to **Hoagies** and cheesesteaks; like traditional hoagies, they are often served to-go, tightly wrapped in wax paper or foil.

If you haven't tried a Vietnamese hoagie,
you're in for a treat.

Bánh Mì

A
B

¼ cup shredded carrots

¼ cup shredded daikon

2 tablespoons sugar

4 tablespoons unseasoned rice vinegar

1 large (20- to 24-inch) French baguette

1 tablespoon fish sauce

1 teaspoon soy sauce

¼ cup mayonnaise

2 to 4 tablespoons chicken or liver pâté, or liverwurst

½ cup very thinly sliced seedless cucumber

½ cup thinly sliced red onion

1 large jalapeño, thinly sliced

2 cooked chicken breasts (about 1½ to 2 pounds total), thinly sliced

10 to 12 sprigs fresh cilantro

❶ In a bowl, combine carrots, daikon, sugar, and vinegar. Toss. Allow to marinate while preparing sandwiches. Preheat oven to 400°F. Place baguette in middle of oven. Toast 10 to 12 minutes, or until warm and crisp.

❷ In a small bowl, combine fish sauce and soy sauce. Slice open toasted baguette. Brush insides with fish sauce mixture, spread mayo and pâté, and then layer cucumber, onion, jalapeño slices, and carrot-daikon mixture. Top with cooked chicken and cilantro sprigs.

❸ Press baguette closed and cut into four equal pieces. **Makes 4**

A
B

Instead of chicken, you can fill a Bánh Mì with pulled pork, boiled shrimp, grilled fish, sautéed tofu, tempeh, or extra vegetables.

BLT

Crisp bacon, cool lettuce, and juicy beefsteak tomatoes

The BLT likely evolved from the British Bacon Butty, or bacon sandwich, a relation of the **Chip Butty**. The earliest record of an American BLT-like sandwich dates to the 1920s. From the 1930s to the '50s, the BLT was a popular item at American lunch counters and diners. Originally a seasonal summer snack, it became a staple after World War II when the expansion of supermarkets made fresh lettuce and tomatoes available year-round. Despite both its age and its humble nature, the BLT remains an American favorite. You can get one practically anywhere: a posh hotel restaurant, a greasy spoon, a school cafeteria, or, best of all, your mom's kitchen.

1 tablespoon mayonnaise
2 slices white bread, preferably toasted
4 slices bacon
2 iceberg or romaine lettuce leaves
2 slices tomato

❶ Spread mayonnaise on bread. Broil or panfry bacon until crisp; drain on a paper towel.

❷ Arrange lettuce and tomato on bread. Top with bacon and close sandwich. Cut in half on the diagonal and serve with potato chips, French fries, or a side of creamy coleslaw. Makes 1

BLT Deluxe

- BLAT: Make this California version of the BLT with bacon, lettuce, avocado, and tomato. Sprinkle fresh sliced avocado with lime juice. Add sprouts if desired.
- BLAST: Add sliced avocado and shrimp.
- BLET: Almost anything tastes better with an egg on top, and the BLT is no exception.
- BLOFT: Add fresh or caramelized onions and feta.

- BLTT: Add smoked turkey and crumbled blue cheese to a basic **BLT** to make this kicked-up Tennessee specialty.
- Salmon BLT: Sandwich seared salmon with crispy bacon, lettuce, and tomato. Top with creamy pesto mayo—one part pesto, one part mayonnaise.

A
B

Bologna Sandwich
A tried-and-true lunch-box favorite

An icon of the American school lunch, a traditional Bologna Sandwich (commonly written and pronounced *baloney*) consists of several pieces of sliced bologna (usually Oscar Mayer brand) on white bread (usually Wonder brand) that is enhanced with a layer of mayonnaise or yellow mustard.

In 1883, German immigrant Oskar Ferdinand Mayer started a meat business in Chicago and, in 1904, began branding its products, which included wieners, bacon, and pork sausage, as Oscar Mayer. In 1948, the company introduced packages of sliced meats that became wildly popular among consumers. With sliced Wonder bread and Oscar Mayer's sliced meats, the American school lunch was never the same again. Homemade sandwiches made from dinner leftovers were gradually replaced by bologna sandwiches that were inexpensive, easily transportable, virtually resistant to spoilage, and fun to eat. Oscar Mayer bologna solidified its enduring popularity with the 1973 jingle "My bologna has a first name"; though the song is more than 35 years old, millions of Americans could probably still recite it on cue. According to Oscar Mayer Inc., approximately 2.19 billion Oscar Mayer bologna sandwiches are eaten each year. That averages out to more than 6 million consumed daily, or 69 sandwiches every second!

---

2 teaspoons mayonnaise or yellow mustard
2 slices white bread, preferably Wonder
3 to 4 slices of bologna, preferably
  Oscar Mayer
Extras, such as American cheese, fresh sliced
  tomato, lettuce, or pickles

Spread mayo or mustard on both slices of bread. Place bologna on bottom piece, add toppings if desired, and close sandwich. For picky eaters, cut off crusts. Makes 1

Serve with a bag of potato chips and a tall glass of milk, seal in a plastic baggie and pack into a lunch box, or cut into cute shapes with cookie cutters.

Bratwurst

The perfect companion to a cold pint

Informally referred to as "brats," these sandwiches consist of German pork sausages that are usually grilled, placed inside a buttered and toasted hard roll, and topped with any number of condiments, especially mustard, pickles, onions, sauerkraut, and shredded cheese. A "double brat" (pronounced "brot") consists of a pair of links.

Germany's love for bratwurst runs deep: The meat has been a part of the German diet since the Middle Ages, and today there are more than 50 regional varieties. In America, bratwurst is most closely associated with the Midwestern states, including Illinois, Ohio, Minnesota, and Wisconsin, which are home to high percentages of German Americans. Brat festivals such as those held in Sheboygan and Madison, Wisconsin, and Bucyrus, Ohio, are enormously popular, drawing thousands of visitors each year. Brats are typically found where crowds are having fun, notably at festivals, amusement parks, baseball stadiums, and Oktoberfests.

The city of Bucyrus stripped Sheboygan of the title "Bratwurst Capital of America" with their winning version: grilled bratwurst on a split rye bun, smothered in sauerkraut, chopped onions, and mustard.

Cooking bratwurst in beer before grilling locks in moisture and helps the meat cook more thoroughly from the inside.

2 uncooked bratwurst sausages (about ¾ pound total)

1 bottle plus 2 ounces good beer, divided

1 tablespoon olive oil, plus more for brushing rolls

1 small yellow onion, thinly sliced

¼ teaspoon sugar

1 teaspoon spicy mustard

2 oblong hard rolls

¼ cup sauerkraut, drained of excess liquid

❶ Preheat grill to medium-high. In a large pot over high heat, cover sausages with 1 bottle of the beer. Just before it reaches a full boil, turn off heat. Remove sausages and place on heated grill. Cook, turning occasionally, until browned and crisp, approximately 12 to 15 minutes, or until interior temperature reaches 160°F.

❷ Warm olive oil in a large skillet over medium-low heat. Add onions and sugar; cook, stirring occasionally, until onions are browned and caramelized, about 10 to 12 minutes. In a small bowl, mix remaining 2 ounces of the beer and mustard until mustard dissolves. Pour over onions; cook over medium heat until sauce is slightly thickened, about 5 minutes.

❸ Slice rolls in half lengthwise. Brush with olive oil and toast on grill 1 to 2 minutes, or until golden and crisp. Scoop sauerkraut onto rolls. Top with cooked sausages and onions. Eat immediately. Makes 2, so you don't have to share

According to most bratwurst aficionados, both yellow mustard and ketchup are anathema. Also, it is law that brats must be washed down with beer. (I don't make the laws, I just report them.) There's even a name for it: *bratwash*. Polka music playing in the background adds kitschy charm and is a must at family gatherings.

Bratwurst

A
B

Breakfast Biscuit Sandwich

A
B

Breakfast Biscuit Sandwich
Buttery delicious breakfast in a biscuit

A flaky, hot-from-the-oven biscuit dabbed with butter and topped with an extra-thick sizzling slice of country ham makes for a delicious breakfast sandwich that's even simpler than the **Classic Breakfast Sandwich**. Although biscuits have been a part of American cuisine since the country's founding, they are the pride and joy of Southerners. Biscuit making underwent a mini-revolution in the mid-1800s with the introduction of commercial leavening agents (baking soda, baking powder, and yeast), which made it easier for home cooks everywhere to pop biscuits in the oven. When the fast-food chain Hardee's opened its doors in 1960, the Breakfast Biscuit Sandwich was here to stay. Today countless varieties can be found in eateries and home kitchens everywhere.

The only dressing this sandwich needs is a smear of butter on the hot biscuit. Of course, a dollop of either spicy or sweet honey mustard works well, too. A side of creamy grits is a great idea, as is a hot mug of strong coffee.

---

1 biscuit, warmed

1 tablespoon butter, divided

2 teaspoons spicy mustard or sweet honey mustard, optional

1 extra-thick slice cooked country ham (about 2 ounces)

❶ Cut biscuit in half. Spread 2 teaspoons of the butter inside. Top with mustard, if desired.

❷ In a small nonstick skillet over medium heat, cook ham 2 to 3 minutes, or until crisp, flipping once. Place on buttered biscuit. Serve hot with remaining butter. Makes 1

Mix 'n' Match!

Bread	*Meat*	*Extras*
Buttermilk biscuits	Bacon	Melted American or cheddar cheese
Cream biscuits	Sausage	Eggs
Jalapeno cheddar biscuits	Chicken-fried steak	Country gravy
	Corned beef hash	

Bresaola and Arugula Sandwich

Cured meat done right

Paper-thin slices of bresaola are typically served on a crusty Italian bread, such as ciabatta, and paired with spicy arugula and extra-virgin olive oil. Bresaola, an air-dried, salted, aged beef that originated in the Valtellina valley region of northern Italy, is treasured for its unique flavor, leanness, and tenderness. Although Italians have been enjoying this meat for centuries, it is a relative newcomer to the United States. Bresaola sandwiches may be found at Italian restaurants, urban bistros, and fine Italian delis, including Venda Ravioli in Providence, Rhode Island. According to one of the restaurant's managers, Chris Spertini, "Bresaola isn't as well known as prosciutto yet, but once people taste it, they love it. The meat is unbelievably tender and full of flavor." He adds, "Since the sandwich is so simple, it's really important to use only the best ingredients you can find."

---

1 teaspoon extra-virgin olive oil
2 thin slices ciabatta bread
5 to 6 paper-thin slices bresaola (4 ounces)
Handful fresh arugula leaves
Sea salt and freshly ground black pepper,
    to taste

❶ Drizzle olive oil on both bread slices. Place bresaola on one slice.

❷ Top with arugula leaves. Sprinkle with sea salt and pepper. Close sandwich and serve.
Makes 1

Imported bresaola is available at Italian specialty
markets, delis, and gourmet markets.

Bresaola and Arugula Sandwich

Caprese Sandwich
Fresh Caprese salad on the go

The simple yet sublime Caprese salad originated on the isle of Capri, in the Campania region of Italy. Inspired by the salad, a Caprese Sandwich is made with alternating layers of fresh, juicy plum tomatoes, creamy buffalo mozzarella cheese, and whole basil leaves tucked inside crusty Italian bread or focaccia that is dressed simply with salt, black pepper, and a liberal drizzling of extra-virgin olive oil.

According to John Brunetto of Mona Lisa Italian Foods in Little Italy, San Diego, a memorable caprese sandwich relies on the freshest ingredients. When possible, use succulent vine-ripened tomatoes (cylindrical plum tomatoes contain fewer seeds than the beefsteak variety) that have never been refrigerated, freshly picked basil, fresh buffalo mozzarella (a semisoft Italian cheese prized for its creamy consistency and mild flavor), and quality extra-virgin olive oil. Despite Mona Lisa's myriad meat-filled sandwiches, Brunetto says the vegetarian Caprese holds its own: "Customers love our Caprese. In fact, it's one of our best sellers."

---

4 slices fresh plum tomato

1 (6-inch) Italian roll, split lengthwise, or 2 thick slices crusty Italian bread

2 ounces fresh buffalo mozzarella, thickly sliced

3 or 4 fresh basil leaves

Salt and freshly ground black pepper, to taste

1 tablespoon extra-virgin olive oil

❶ Arrange tomato slices slightly overlapping on roll. Place overlapping mozzarella slices on top of tomatoes. Add basil.

❷ Season with salt and pepper. Drizzle with olive oil. Close sandwich and serve. Makes 1

For variety, whisk extra-virgin olive oil with aged balsamic vinegar and minced garlic, substitute freshly prepared arugula or basil pesto for the basil, or add 2 to 3 slices of prosciutto.

Chicken Cutlet Sandwich

Crunchy hot chicken with melted cheese

The Chicken Cutlet Sandwich, sometimes pronounced "sangwich" by Italian Americans, is a mainstay on the menus of delis, pizza parlors, and mom-and-pop eateries. It consists of breaded white chicken that's fried or baked and then served on a bun or long roll. Popular toppings include provolone or buffalo mozzarella cheese, hot peppers, pesto, and sautéed broccoli rabe. These Italian-style sandwiches were introduced by immigrants from that country at the turn of the twentieth century in cities with large existing immigrant populations, namely Philadelphia, New York, and Chicago.

You can substitute veal cutlets for chicken; combine chicken cutlets with sliced fresh buffalo mozzarella and roasted red bell peppers or hot Italian peppers; spread a layer of basil pesto on the bread; or add olive-oil-soaked sun-dried tomatoes and sliced fresh buffalo mozzarella.

Broccoli rabe, also known as rapini, looks like slender broccoli and has a sharp, slightly bitter flavor.

Chicken Cutlet Sandwich

CRUNCHY CHICKEN CUTLETS

2 eggs

2 tablespoons milk

⅛ teaspoon crushed red pepper flakes

⅛ teaspoon salt

¼ cup all-purpose flour

⅔ cup plain bread crumbs

3 tablespoons olive oil

4 (4- to 6-ounce) chicken cutlets,
  about ½ inch thick

SAUTÉED BROCCOLI RABE

1 bunch broccoli rabe, stems removed

2 cloves garlic, finely chopped

1 tablespoon olive oil

¼ teaspoon crushed red pepper flakes

½ teaspoon salt

4 torpedo or ciabatta rolls, split lengthwise

8 slices provolone cheese

❶ In a wide shallow bowl, whisk together eggs, milk, red pepper, and salt. Place flour in a separate shallow bowl; do the same for bread crumbs. In a large skillet over medium heat, warm olive oil. One at a time, dip chicken cutlets into flour and then egg mixture, allowing excess to drip off. Dredge in bread crumbs, coating evenly. Cook 3 to 4 minutes on each side, or until golden brown and crisp. Place on a paper-towel-lined dish.

❷ Bring a large saucepan of salted water to a boil. Boil broccoli rabe 2 minutes; drain and plunge into a bowl of ice water. ("Shocking" the broccoli rabe in this way preserves its vivid green color.) In a large skillet over medium heat, sauté garlic in olive oil until it starts to turn golden. Add broccoli rabe, red pepper, and salt. Sauté 1 to 2 minutes more, until broccoli rabe is just tender.

❸ Place a chicken cutlet on each roll. Top each with broccoli rabe and 2 cheese slices. Broil 1 to 2 minutes, or until cheese melts, and serve immediately. Makes 4

C
D

Chicken-Fried Steak Sandwich

Texas on a bun

C
D

This sandwich consists of a hulking piece of battered fried steak on a hamburger bun, garnished with lettuce, tomato, mayonnaise, and pickles or a ladleful of cream gravy. Like its home state of Texas, chicken-fried steak is *big*: big in size, big on flavor, big in popularity. Introduced to North America in the mid-nineteenth century by German immigrants who settled in central Texas, it is a spinoff of German weiner schnitzel (thin bread-crumb-coated pieces of veal that are fried). It likely developed as a way to make tough, inexpensive cuts of meat more appetizing. Despite its name, chicken-fried steak contains no chicken. Rather, the "fried" refers to the cooking process, which, as for Southern fried chicken, consists of pieces of tenderized meat dredged in flour or dipped in batter and fried until golden.

It is an unofficial yet widely acknowledged Texas law that every plate of chicken-fried steak must be drowned in rich cream gravy. When it comes to the sandwiches, however, gravy is optional. Many restaurants serve them adorned simply with a slice of American or cheddar cheese.

CHICKEN-FRIED STEAK

1 (4- to 6-ounce) round steak

1 egg

2 tablespoons whole milk or buttermilk

Several shakes of salt and freshly ground
   black pepper, to taste

¼ teaspoon paprika

2 tablespoons all-purpose flour

2 tablespoons canola oil

CREAM GRAVY

1 tablespoon all-purpose flour

¼ cup milk

Salt and freshly ground black pepper, to taste

1 hamburger bun or kaiser roll, sliced open

❶ Trim steak of fat. Using the flat side of a meat mallet, pound meat until ⅛ inch thick. In a small bowl, whisk together egg, milk, salt, pepper, and paprika. Place flour in a shallow plate. Heat oil in a large skillet over medium heat. Dip meat into egg mixture, then dredge in flour. Repeat. Place in hot oil. Fry 3 to 4 minutes; flip once and fry 2 to 3 minutes, or until crisp and golden brown.

❷ For the cream gravy, scoop 1 tablespoon of oil from the skillet in which the meat was cooked and add it to a small pan over medium-high heat. Whisk in flour, then gradually whisk in milk. Season with salt and pepper. Lower heat and continue whisking until sauce thickens. (It should cling to the back of the spoon.) For a thinner sauce, add more milk; for a thicker sauce, add more flour.

❸ Place steak on sliced bun and top gener-ously with cream gravy. Serve with crispy French fries or onion rings or, for a more Southern feel, add a side of black-eyed peas or mashed potatoes. Makes 1

Chicken Salad Sandwich

The easy everyday feast

It's hard to believe that the unassuming Chicken Salad Sandwich, so prevalent on the menus of many a humble establishment, was once considered a lavish meal. But it's true: Some of the earliest recipes date back to the 1880s, when steep chicken prices made it a meal for only the wealthy. It wasn't until after World War II, when chicken prices decreased significantly, that it became a favorite of middle-class households. With the increased availability of sliced bread and store-bought mayonnaise, chicken salad sandwiches became both a dependable brown-bag lunch and an easy dinner.

The sandwich consists of chopped or shredded cooked chicken that is mixed with creamy mayonnaise and chopped raw vegetables; holding it all together are two slices of toasted white or wheat bread. Popular add-ins include capers, gherkins, olives, sweet relish, and fresh dill.

Chicken salad holds a special place in the South. And the following recipe—courtesy of the famed Loveless Café in Nashville, Tennessee—is no exception. According to owner Jesse Goldstein, "We are famous for our fried chicken and country ham and biscuits, but our guests have developed quite a hunger for chicken salad, too. Everyone loves its not-to-sweet, old-fashioned flavor. To make it extra-Southern, sprinkle in toasted pecans for a good nutty crunch."

You've gotta respect the chicken: Using a moderate amount
of mayonnaise will add smoothness to the salad without
masking the chicken's flavor and texture.

Chicken Salad Sandwich

About 4 cups (2 1/2 pounds) diced cooked
    chicken
1 cup finely diced celery
1/2 cup relish
1 cup mayonnaise
3/4 cup dried cranberries
1/2 Vidalia onion, finely diced (about 1/2 cup)
1 teaspoon salt
1 teaspoon freshly ground black pepper
1 cup pecan pieces, optional
8 slices white or whole-grain bread

❶ Combine chicken salad ingredients in a
bowl. Cover and chill at least 2 hours to let
flavors meld.

❷ To make each sandwich scoop about 3/4 to
1 cup chicken salad onto a slice of toasted or
untoasted bread and top with a second slice of
bread. Makes 4

C
D

Chip Butty

Everybody's best buddy

Whether or not you appreciate traditional British cuisine, it's hard not to like the tasty chip butty, also known as chip sandwiches across Britain, breadcakes in Sheffield, piece-n-chips in Scotland, or French fry sandwiches elsewhere. *Butty* is a Welsh term for "sandwich" and slang for "friend" or "buddy." It's not surprising that this is one of the most beloved sandwiches in the United Kingdom, especially in the north. After a long night out on the town, a Chip Butty might just be your best friend, too.

This working-class, vegetarian-friendly sandwich consists simply of bread, butter, and fries that melt the butter; condiments such as ketchup, malt vinegar, brown gravy, and cheese sauce are all acceptable and encouraged. Just not all at the same time.

A few tablespoons butter
2 slices white bread
¾ to 1 cup hot French fries

Liberally butter both slices of bread. Fill with French fries. If you'd like, season with salt and pepper. Eat it quickly, while it's hot! Makes 1

There's a Butty for Every Buddy

- Bacon Butty: Replace fries with bacon to make this British relative of the BLT.
- Scallop Butty: Batter fries before frying.

- Horseshoe: To make this American version invented in Springfield, Illinois, dump fries over an open-faced sandwich and smother in cheese sauce.

C
D

Chopped Liver Sandwich

What am I, chopped liver?

Chopped liver is a spread made of ground livers, usually beef or chicken (or both), mixed with schmaltz (rendered chicken fat), chopped hard-boiled eggs, and onions. It's a staple of American Jewish cuisine that was created as a way to prevent waste and use all parts of the animal, including organs. Some people like to pair chopped liver with other classic Jewish sandwich meats, such as corned beef or pastrami; however, purists prefer it alone to better appreciate its unique flavor. A Chopped Liver Sandwich traditionally consists of chopped liver spread liberally between two slices of rye bread. Perhaps the most famous place to get an authentic chopped liver sandwich is Katz's Delicatessen in New York City.

Prepared chopped liver is available at Jewish delis and markets. You can make your own schmaltz. But if you're not keen on doing so, or are looking for a quick chopped-liver fix (and don't mind a slightly less flavorful result), substitute peanut oil or butter (the latter only if you're not kosher).

About 6 tablespoons peanut oil
1 large yellow onion, diced
1 pound chicken livers
¼ teaspoon salt
¼ teaspoon freshly ground black pepper
2 hard-boiled eggs, cooled, peeled, and
    coarsely chopped
8 slices seeded rye or marble rye bread,
    lightly toasted
A few thin slices white onion, optional

❶ Warm oil in a large skillet over medium-low heat. Add diced onions and sauté 10 to 15 minutes, or until tender and translucent.

❷ Rinse chicken livers and pat dry; trim of excess fat. Increase heat to medium and add livers to skillet, seasoning generously with salt and pepper. Cook 8 to 10 minutes, or until tender and just barely pink in the center.

❸ Transfer mixture to a food processor. Pulse several times; it should be slightly chunky yet spreadable. Pour mixture into a bowl. Stir in eggs and season to taste with salt and pepper. Chill in an airtight container 1 to 2 hours. Spread liberally onto bread. Garnish with onion slices, if desired. Eat. Makes 4

Chow Mein Sandwich

The #1 sandwich for noodle lovers

If the Oriental Chow Mein Company in Fall River, Massachusetts, hadn't opened in 1936, this concoction of hot chow mein and crispy fried egg noodles served on an untoasted hamburger bun might never have existed. Their crunchy fried noodles have been the star ingredient of this regional specialty for decades. Found primarily in southeastern Massachusetts and parts of Rhode Island, a Chow Mein Sandwich is a culinary oddity: It's less a sandwich and more a bowl of chow mein with a hamburger bun. Diners love it because it's filling, inexpensive, and completely original. Evelyn's Drive-In in Tiverton, Rhode Island, serves the real deal. As co-owner Jane Bitto explains, "We make our sandwiches only with Chow Mein Company's noodles. That's the way Evelyn, the original owner, made them, and that's the way we still do it today. And customers just love it. . . . It's like a taste from the past."

Gravy Master or Kitchen Bouquet can be found in the spice or gravy section of most major supermarkets. Oriental Chow Mein Company noodles can be ordered online. For an even quicker sandwich, purchase packaged chow mein mix and follow the instructions. This recipe is slightly adapted from an original provided by Jane Bitto.

---

2 yellow onions, cut into small wedges

2 stalks celery, thinly sliced (use all parts of the stalk)

½ cup mung bean sprouts

4 cups chicken broth, divided

¼ cup cornstarch

1 tablespoon Gravy Master or Kitchen Bouquet

1 beef bouillon cube, dissolved in 1 cup water

Salt and pepper, to taste

4 hamburger buns, halved lengthwise

1 pound Oriental Chow Mein Company noodles (or other crispy noodle of your choice)

❶ In a large pot over medium-high heat, stir together onions, celery, and sprouts. In a small bowl, combine 1 cup of the chicken broth with cornstarch; stir until dissolved. Add to vegetables. Add the remaining 3 cups chicken broth, Gravy Master, dissolved beef bouillon, salt, and pepper. Bring to a boil. Lower heat and cook until vegetables are tender and sauce has thickened, about 8 to 10 minutes.

❷ To serve, open hamburger buns and add a handful of noodles to each side. Ladle chow mein on top and serve immediately. Don't forget the silverware and lots of napkins. Makes 4

Clam Roll

A crispy golden summertime sandwich

The modest Clam Roll is often upstaged by its more glamorous cousin, the **Lobster Roll**. When prepared well, however, the Clam Roll can steal the show. It consists of a toasted bun overflowing with crisp, golden fried clams (bellies included), accompanied by lemon wedges and hot sauce—not to mention a side of French fries or coleslaw.

This decidedly New England dish began appearing on menus in the 1800s, most commonly at mom-and-pop restaurants and small roadside shacks that dot the coast. Most recipes specify strips, which refer to slices of hard-shell clam, and bellies, which refer to whole soft-shell clams. Aficionados say the bellies are superior in both taste and texture. Strips are crispy; bellies have a crisp exterior but a squishy, sweet center that pops in your mouth when you bite them. The choice is yours.

3 to 4 cups canola or peanut oil for frying
¼ cup evaporated milk
1 egg, lightly beaten
A few splashes hot sauce, plus more for serving
¾ teaspoon salt
¾ teaspoon freshly ground black pepper
¼ cup cornmeal
¼ cup all-purpose flour
10 to 12 whole soft-shell clams with bellies, shucked, rinsed, and drained
2 split-top buns, buttered and toasted
¼ cup tartar sauce
4 lemon wedges

❶ Fill a small, deep saucepan 2 to 3 inches deep with oil and preheat to 350°F. In a small bowl, whisk together evaporated milk, egg, hot sauce, salt, and pepper. In a shallow bowl or plate, combine cornmeal and flour. Dip clams in egg mixture, allowing excess to drip into the bowl. Dredge in cornmeal-flour mixture until completely coated.

❷ Carefully fry a few at a time 3 to 4 minutes, or until golden brown and crisp. Remove with a slotted spoon and place on a paper-towel-lined plate. Repeat with remaining clams.

❸ Pile clams into buns. Top with tartar sauce and serve with hot sauce and lemon wedges on the side. Makes 4

Classic Breakfast Sandwich
The breakfast of champions

As the name implies, a breakfast sandwich is quite simply one that is served for breakfast, and this variation is among the most popular: a toasted English muffin filled with tender cooked eggs, crisp bacon, and melted cheese. The most famous breakfast sandwich is the granddaddy of them all, the Egg McMuffin, which was invented in 1972 by Herb Peterson, co-owner of a McDonald's in Santa Barbara, California. Peterson wanted to introduce breakfast items to the chain restaurant, so he came up with a "crazy idea—a breakfast sandwich." Turns out it wasn't so crazy after all. Peterson's original Egg McMuffin—a griddle-steamed egg formed in a Teflon circle, topped with Canadian bacon and American cheese, and served open-faced on a toasted and buttered English muffin—was an instant hit with diners. Its phenomenal success wowed McDonald's executives as well as founder Ray Kroc, who ultimately decided to make breakfast a fixture on the chain's menu. To create a perfectly circular egg, purchase an egg ring. Or use the smallest skillet you can find and just don't worry. Even lopsided eggs taste delicious.

About 2 tablespoons butter, divided
1 English muffin, split open
2 slices bacon
2 eggs, lightly beaten
Salt and pepper to taste
1 slice American or cheddar cheese

❶ Lightly butter English muffin and toast in a skillet until crisp and golden brown. In a non-stick skillet over medium heat, cook bacon 2 to 3 minutes, or until crisp, flipping once.

❷ Melt remaining butter in a skillet over medium heat. Add eggs, season with salt and pepper, and cook 2 minutes, or until slightly puffed. Flip and cook 1 more minute.

❸ Place cheese on bottom of muffin. Top with 1 slice bacon, then eggs, then second bacon slice. Close sandwich and serve hot. Makes 1

C
D

Classic Club

Open wide!

This tall toasted triple-decker is tidily constructed with chicken (or turkey or ham), bacon, lettuce, tomato, and mayonnaise and then cut into four triangles that are then secured with cocktail picks. The number of layers is a matter of personal choice, but overstuffing quickly turns a club sandwich into a **Dagwood**. Sliced chicken can be replaced or supplemented with turkey, ham, or roast beef and accompanied by a slice of American, cheddar, or Swiss cheese. These variations typically go by the name of the featured meat, such as a turkey or ham club.

The Classic Club debuted in 1894 at a New York gentlemen's club called the Saratoga Club House. Most historians agree that the original sandwich was made with sliced chicken and modeled after the double-decker club cars on early-twentieth-century trains; today, hefty triple-deckers are commonplace. Legendary American chef and food writer James Beard had this to say about them: "Whoever started that horror should be forced to eat three-deckers three times a day the rest of his life."

---

3 slices white bread, with or without crusts

1 tablespoon mayonnaise

2 lettuce leaves (romaine or iceberg)

4 thin slices tomato

4 slices cooked bacon

4 ounces cooked chicken breast, thinly sliced

4 cocktail sticks

❶ Toast bread until crisp. Spread mayo on one side of each slice. Take first slice, mayo side up, and top with 1 lettuce leaf and 2 tomato slices. Neatly layer 2 bacon slices and half the chicken on top. Cover with second toast slice, mayo side up. Continue with remaining fillings. Top with third toast slice, mayo side down.

❷ Secure layers with cocktail sticks, making sure they reach to the bottom of the sandwich. Using a serrated knife, cut diagonally into 4 triangles. Makes 1

Serve this classic gentleman's sandwich with French fries or potato chips and a pickle.

Crab Melt

Broiled to cheesey, toasty perfection

More than 1.5 million pounds of crab are consumed worldwide each year. Since there are thousands of crab varieties, culinary preferences for the crustacean vary significantly. In America there are distinct regional favorites, such as blue crab in the Chesapeake Bay, Dungeness crab in the Pacific Northwest, and rock crab in Maine. Just about all regions, however, have their own version of the easygoing Crab Melt. Usually served open-faced, it is constructed with toasted, buttered bread and a spread of moist, sweet crab salad topped with melted Swiss or cheddar cheese.

The crab salad can be made ahead of time and refrigerated in an airtight container for 2 to 3 days. Just don't add the onions until you're ready to eat. Try serving this sandwich on a toasted English muffin instead of Texas toast. For a California twist, substitute cheddar cheese for the Swiss and parsley for the dill, and then add sliced avocado, red onions, and sprouts.

---

2 slices Texas toast
1 tablespoon butter
8 ounces fresh or canned lump crabmeat
3 to 4 tablespoons mayonnaise
½ teaspoon lemon juice
¼ cup diced celery
1 tablespoon chopped scallions
1 tablespoon chopped fresh dill
Salt and freshly ground black pepper, to taste
4 slices Swiss cheese

❶ Preheat broiler. Toast and butter bread. In a medium bowl, combine all remaining ingredients except cheese. Mix until thick and creamy.

❷ Divide crab mixture evenly between bread slices. Top each with 2 cheese slices. Broil 2 to 3 minutes, or until cheese begins to bubble and melt. Serve warm. Makes 1

Pairs well with a cold beer and
a side of crispy hot sweet-potato fries.

Croissant Sandwich

Buttery, flaky crescents filled with goodness

The croissant, a national symbol of France, was traditionally eaten only at breakfast. According to Alan Davidson in *The Oxford Companion to Food*, things changed in the 1970s with the advent of *le fast food*. To slow the burgeoning popularity of the American **Hamburger**, the French created *croissanteries*, small eateries that serve Croissant Sandwiches at breakfast or lunch. Popular breakfast fillings include eggs, cheese, bacon, and ham; sliced deli meats and salads, such as chicken, egg, or seafood, are lunchtime favorites.

This recipe makes a classic smoked salmon and dill croissant; smoked salmon is widely available at seafood markets as well as most major supermarkets. You can fill croissants with anything you like, from melted cheese to sweet jam and chocolate.

SMOKED SALMON SALAD

4 ounces smoked salmon, cut into bite-size
   pieces
1 tablespoon finely chopped scallions
¼ cup thinly sliced celery
2 tablespoons mayonnaise (regular or light)
1 tablespoon plain yogurt or sour cream
1 teaspoon lemon juice
2 teaspoons Dijon mustard
2 teaspoons finely chopped fresh dill
Salt and freshly ground black pepper, to taste

1 croissant, halved lengthwise
3 to 4 thin slices cucumber, optional
2 to 3 thin slices avocado, optional

❶ In a small bowl, combine salmon, scallions, and celery; toss gently. In a separate small bowl, whisk together remaining salad ingredients. Pour over salmon mixture and gently stir until well combined. This salad can be eaten at room temperature. If you prefer it chilled, refrigerate in an airtight container at least 30 minutes (or up to 1 day) prior to serving.

❷ Open croissant and fill with salmon salad. Add cucumber or avocado, if desired. Makes 1

Croque-Monsieur

Hot ham and cheese, French-style

Loosely translated as "Mister Crunch" or "Mister Crisp," the beloved Croque-Monsieur was likely an accidental creation. According to popular legend, French workers left their lunch tins containing ham and cheese sandwiches near hot radiators. When lunchtime rolled around, they discovered the cheese had melted and—*voilà!*—the Croque-Monsieur was born. No one knows who had the brilliant idea to fry or grill the sandwich in clarified butter, the mark of a genuine Croque-Monsieur, which first appeared on a Paris café menu in 1910. Over time, another popular preparation method evolved: dipping the sandwich in an egg mixture (page 61) and then frying it in butter, like the **Monte Cristo**.

Today the Croque-Monsieur, typically shortened to "croque," is widely available at French cafés and bars and is enjoyed as an appetizer, a satisfying snack, or a light main meal. It tastes best when eaten in an outdoor Paris café with an attractive companion. If you can't get to the City of Light, simply enjoy yours with a hot bowl of creamy tomato soup or a side salad. Not as romantic, but definitely just as delicious.

About 2 tablespoons butter or clarified butter (page 61), divided

2 slices white bread

Dijon mustard, optional

2 thin slices baked or boiled ham

¼ cup grated or 2 thin slices Gruyère cheese

Salt and freshly ground black pepper, to taste

❶ Butter both slices of bread. If using mustard, spread it on one side of each bread slice. Top one slice, mustard-side up, with ham, then cheese. Season to taste with salt and pepper. Top with other bread slice, mustard side down.

❷ Melt remaining butter in a griddle or frying pan over medium-high heat. Fry sandwich about 3 minutes per side, or until crisp and golden brown. (If you prefer not to fry the sandwich on the stove top, broil 1 to 2 minutes per side, until crisp and golden brown.) Serve hot. Makes 1

There's More Than One Way to Make a Mr. Crisp

- Barros Jarpa: Use ham and Monterey Jack cheese to make this variation, popular in Chile.
- Barros Luco: Substitute roast beef for ham.
- Croque-Auvergnat: Substitute blue cheese for Gruyère.
- Croque-Madame: Serve a Croque-Monsieur with a fried egg on top to make a Croque-Madame, aka Mrs. Crisp.
- Croque-Norvégien: Replace ham with smoked salmon.
- Croque-Provençal: Add sliced tomato.
- Croque-Monsieur with Béchamel: For a special meal, serve a Croque-Monsieur bathed in a rich and creamy béchamel (a basic white sauce).
- Francesinha: Also known as "Little Frenchie," this sandwich is a Portuguese take on the Croque-Monsieur, made with ham and Portuguese sausage and then smothered in melted cheese and a beer sauce.

In France, McDonald's serves a crispy fried sandwich called a Croque McDo.

Clarified Butter

Here's how to make clarified butter, or *beurre noisette,* which gives sandwiches like the Croque-Monsieur an extra rich flavor. This simple process removes the milk solids and water so that the butter can retain its rich flavor and cook to a higher temperature without burning.

1 stick (½ cup) unsalted butter

❶ In a medium saucepan over low heat, completely melt butter. A white froth will form on the top; carefully skim it off. Let cool; the milk solids will settle on the bottom.

❷ Strain the mixture through a fine sieve or cheesecloth into a glass bowl. The golden yellow liquid that seeps through the sieve is the clarified butter. If stored in an airtight container and refrigerated, clarified butter will last up to 3 to 4 weeks. Makes 6 tablespoons

Egg Mixture

For a classic Parisian sandwich, dip your Croque-Monsieur in this simple egg mixture before frying.

2 eggs
¼ teaspoon salt
⅛ teaspoon black pepper

❶ Whisk together eggs, salt, pepper, and 1 tablespoon water.

❷ After assembling sandwiches, dip each in egg mixture prior to frying in butter. Makes enough for 4 sandwiches

C
D

Cubano

The classic Cuban pressed sandwich

A good Cubano consists of *lechón asado*, pork loin roasted with a *mojo* marinade; *jamon dulce*, a succulent sweet-cured ham; and lots of Swiss cheese, yellow mustard, and sliced pickles packed securely into a small loaf of crusty Cuban bread. This sandwich is traditionally toasted and flattened by a press called a *plancha* until the meats and cheese melt into gooey perfection.

In the late 1800s, Cuban immigrants working in Florida's first cigar factories and sugar mills routinely brought Cubanos for lunch. It is impossible to ascertain whether the sandwich was a distinctly Cuban or Cuban American creation. Most food historians agree that it's the result of several ethnic cuisines: The Cubans introduced the *mojo*, the Spanish introduced the ham, the Cuban Americans introduced the fixins, and the Italians introduced the salami found in some variations. By the early 1900s, Cuban sandwiches were offered in cafés, cafeterias, and mom-and-pop restaurants throughout Cuba and Ybor City, Florida. Although many consider the Cubano part of Miami's culinary history, aficionados are quick to point out that Ybor City holds the distinct honor of being this sandwich's home. Locals there agree that the most delicious and authentic ones are bought at *loncherías*, small inexpensive street-corner snack bars.

This authentic recipe is reprinted with permission from *Three Guys from Miami Cook Cuban* by Glenn Mo Lindgren, Raúl Musibay, and Jorge Castillo—three guys who love their Cubanos.

The home cook needn't purchase a *plancha* to achieve the classic flattened form. Simply use a panini press or place the sandwich in a hot cast-iron skillet and cover with a heavy weight—a pan or a tin-foil-wrapped brick—as it cooks.

4 loaves Cuban bread
A few tablespoons butter
Sliced dill pickles
1 pound lechón asado (opposite)
1 pound sliced sweet-cured ham
½ pound mild Swiss cheese
Yellow mustard, optional

❶ Preheat a lightly greased pancake griddle or large frying pan. Slice bread into sections about 8 inches long. Cut these in half lengthwise and spread butter inside. Add pickles, lechón asado, ham, and cheese. Be generous! If using mustard, add before closing sandwich.

❷ Place sandwich on the hot pan and flatten it, compressing bread to about one-third its original size. Grill 2 or 3 minutes on each side, until cheese is melted and bread is golden. Slice sandwich in half on the diagonal and serve hot. Makes 4

The After-Party Cubano

- Medianoche: Serve a Cubano on small sweet bread, such as egg bread or Jewish challah.

As its name suggests (*medianoche* is Spanish for "midnight"), this slightly sweet version of the Cubano is a popular late-night snack eaten after an evening of dancing or partying.

Lechón Asado

Mojo is a decidedly Cuban marinade made with sour orange juice (or two parts orange juice to one part lemon juice and one part lime juice); it gives *lechón asado* its distinct flavor. Mojo roast pork can be purchased at major supermarkets and Cuban and Mexican specialty markets or made from scratch using this recipe. You'll need only about a pound for the Cubano recipe; the rest can be refrigerated or frozen for later use.

1 head garlic
1 teaspoon salt
1 teaspoon black peppercorns
1 cup sour orange juice
1 cup minced onion
2 teaspoons dried oregano
½ cup Spanish olive oil
1 (2- to 4-pound) pork shoulder roast or pork loin roast

❶ Using a mortar and pestle, mash garlic, salt, and peppercorns into a paste. Stir in sour orange juice, onion, and oregano. Let rest at room temperature for 30 minutes.

❷ Heat olive oil in a 2-quart saucepan until hot (about 220°F). Remove from heat and quickly whisk in orange-juice mixture. Let cool.

❸ Pierce pork roast several times with a sharp knife or fork. Pour garlic mixture overtop (save a little for basting while roasting), cover, and refrigerate 2 to 3 hours.

❹ Using a suitable roasting pan or rack, sprinkle remaining marinade over pork and cook uncovered at 325°F. Basting occasionally, roast about 20 minutes per pound until completely cooked (160°F).

❺ Bring pan juices to a boil and simmer until reduced by half. Pour over the pork after you put it in the sandwich. Makes enough for about 15 sandwiches

C
D

Curried Chicken Salad Sandwich

A sandwich fit for a queen

A Curried Chicken Salad Sandwich is distinguished from a traditional **Chicken Salad Sandwich** by the addition of aromatic curry powder and such add-ins as fresh mango, apricots, raisins, carrots, and cashews. It can be served on many kinds of toasted bread, from sourdough or white to wheat or raisin walnut.

Curried chicken salad became the chicken salad par excellence when it graced the table of Queen Elizabeth's coronation luncheon in 1953. The multitalented Constance Spry, who created the floral arrangements for the coronation, invented this elegant salad. (Her version was made with wine and apricot jam.) If you never receive an invitation to Buckingham Palace, you can still find this delicious sandwich at eateries ranging from posh restaurants to casual diners. Even Dodger Stadium in Los Angeles introduced a low-fat curried chicken salad to its menu in 2009. Of course, you'll have to bring your own bread.

You can substitute ¼ cup diced dried apricots for the mango, or add ½ cup halved seedless red grapes. Queen Elizabeth would approve.

CURRIED CHICKEN AND MANGO SALAD

2 cups cooked, shredded chicken breast
    (about ½ pound)

¼ cup diced and peeled carrot

½ cup diced mild-flavored apple with skin, such
    as Fuji or Gala, sprinkled with lemon juice

1 small ripe mango, peeled and diced

2 scallions, thinly sliced

¼ cup coarsely chopped cashews

2 tablespoons raisins

¼ cup mayonnaise

⅓ cup plain yogurt

1 teaspoon apple cider vinegar

1 teaspoon minced fresh ginger

2 teaspoons curry powder

⅛ teaspoon cayenne pepper

⅛ teaspoon salt

4 slices toasted bread of your choice,
    such as sourdough, whole wheat, white,
    or raisin walnut

❶ In a bowl, mix together chicken, carrot, apple, mango, scallions, cashews, and raisins. In a separate bowl, whisk together remaining salad ingredients until smooth and creamy.

❷ Pour dressing over chicken mixture, stirring until well coated. Refrigerate in an airtight container at least 2 to 3 hours before serving; it tastes best chilled.

❸ Place toasted bread on a clean work surface. Divide chicken salad evenly between 2 slices. Close sandwiches and cut each in half on the diagonal. Makes 2

C
D

Curried Chicken Salad Sandwich

Dagwood

Everything but the kitchen sink

The original version of this colossal multilayered sandwich included the questionable combination of sardines and baked beans; today it is constructed with any combination of cold cuts, vegetables, and condiments. There is no correct way to build a Dagwood; it's up to the maker to pile on as many favorite fillings as possible without toppling the food-stuffed tower.

The sandwich was the creation of cartoonist Murat "Chic" Young, who introduced it in his comic strip *Blondie* in 1936. He showed Dagwood Bumstead, the quintessential bumbling husband, raiding the refrigerator to create a soaring sandwich composed of everything but the kitchen sink. Americans gobbled up the humor, and the sandwich became a regular feature of the cartoon character's daily life as well as their own. Today there is even a franchise called Dagwood's Sandwich Shoppes that, according to their Web site, targets "heavy sandwich users."

In order to create a mountainous masterpiece, try piercing the middle of the sandwich with a long toothpick or wooden skewer. If you're all out of toothpicks or just really hungry, try what Dagwood did in one cartoon: pierce the sandwich with a frankfurter. Make sure you have a really big, cold drink to wash it down.

---

❶ Open your refrigerator and find the following items:

- As many slices of your favorite bread as you can eat
- As many slices of your favorite meats and cheese as you'd like
- Any desired fillers, such as lettuce, tomatoes, pickles, or peppers
- As many condiments, such as mustard, mayo, BBQ sauce, or Thousand Island dressing, as you can manage
- A really long toothpick or wooden skewer
- A green olive

❷ Spread out all ingredients on a large, clean work surface. If you're married, make sure your spouse isn't around. Carefully build your sandwich, enjoying every minute. Pierce it with the toothpick or skewer. Stick the olive on the top.

❸ Pour yourself a big tall glass of your favorite cold beverage and place it next to the sandwich. Stretch your jaws a few times, take a deep breath of satisfaction, and open wide.

Makes 1

The-Day-After-Thanksgiving Turkey Sandwich

A feast between sliced bread

What is America's favorite way to eat leftover Thanksgiving turkey? You guessed it: in a sandwich. Thick slabs of toasted white bread can be piled high with leftover turkey meat, mashed potatoes or stuffing, cranberry sauce, and brown gravy.

The November celebration that began at a single table nearly 400 years ago has grown into a holiday feast eaten in more than 90 percent of American households. According to the National Turkey Federation, Americans gobble more than 690 million pounds of the big bird every Thanksgiving. Closed or open faced, hot or cold, there's more than one way to fit a banquet into a sandwich.

---

1 tablespoon mayonnaise
2 thick slices white bread, preferably Texas toast
2 thick slices leftover roasted turkey
¼ cup mashed potatoes or stuffing (or both)
1 to 2 tablespoons cranberry sauce
1 to 2 tablespoons brown gravy

Spread mayo on both slices of bread. Place turkey slices on one piece of bread. Top with potatoes and/or stuffing, cranberry sauce, and brown gravy. Close sandwich. Slice in half and eat immediately. Makes 1

Let's Talk Turkey

- Barbecue Turkey Sandwich: Top turkey with barbecue sauce and cooked bacon strips; melt cheddar cheese on top.
- The Pilgrim: Pile roasted turkey, stuffing, cranberry sauce, gravy, and Muenster cheese on white bread.

- Turkey Melt: Arrange turkey on toast, top with Swiss or cheddar cheese, and broil until cheese melts.

The-Day-After-Thanksgiving Turkey Sandwich

C
D

Denver Sandwich

Hearty Rocky Mountain fare

As with the Old West itself, this sandwich's origins can be traced back to several legends. Food historians agree that the Denver, or "Western," Sandwich surfaced sometime during the nineteenth century among settlers on westward pioneer treks. After that, the story gets a bit muddied. Some believe that adding onions to spoiled eggs helped mask their unappetizing taste and smell, and that this combination led to the creation of this sandwich. Others claim that pioneer women and chuck-wagon cooks created the omelet as a nourishing snack for cowboys to carry in their saddlebags. But American chef and author James Beard claims that Chinese cooks working for logging camps and railroad gangs invented it as an Americanized version of egg foo young. Ever popular, it can still be found at high- and low-end eateries throughout the United States, where it goes by a few names: "Western" in states east of the Mississippi and "Denver" in most of the rest of the country. But many diners simply call it a "cowboy."

About 2 tablespoons butter, divided
4 thick slices white or whole wheat bread
¼ cup finely chopped yellow onion
¼ cup chopped green bell pepper
¼ cup diced cooked ham
4 eggs
1 tablespoon milk
¼ teaspoon salt
¼ teaspoon freshly ground black pepper

❶ Butter and toast bread with 2 teaspoons of the butter; set aside. Melt remaining butter in a small (8-inch) nonstick skillet over medium heat. Add onion, peppers, and ham, and sauté until vegetables are tender and ham is lightly browned. In a bowl, whisk together eggs, milk, salt, and pepper. Slowly pour over vegetables.

❷ Cook 2 to 3 minutes, or until eggs begin to solidify and a crust forms around the edges, gently stirring egg mixture as it cooks.

❸ When eggs are nearly done, split omelet down the middle. Flip and cook 1 to 2 minutes more, or until eggs are set and lightly browned. Place each half omelet on toasted bread. Close sandwiches and serve. Makes 2

Deviled Ham Sandwich

Star of the ladies' luncheon

So-called deviled foods are those prepared with hot seasonings, such as cayenne pepper and dry mustard. (And, yes, the name refers to the mythical red-hot horned beast from hell.) Deviled Ham Sandwiches are typically bite-size concoctions of ground cooked ham mixed with any variety of seasonings and condiments—cayenne pepper, spicy mustard, chopped pickle, mayonnaise—and spread between bread.

Created in 1868, deviled ham was the front-runner of all deviled products sold by the William Underwood Company. Underwood, who founded the business in 1822, helped make this sandwich spread wildly popular throughout much of the nineteenth and twentieth centuries. Despite its longstanding role as a perennial star of ladies' luncheons and buffets, in the last few decades the Deviled Ham Sandwich has lost much of its luster. Spice up deviled ham salad with other condiments (like Dijon mustard) and fresh add-ins, such as chopped gherkins or celery. For a buffet, spread deviled ham salad on finger rolls. Or make canapés by slicing off the crusts of white or whole wheat bread and cutting the sandwiches into finger-length rectangles.

---

2 cups chopped or ground cooked ham
¼ cup sweet pickle relish
⅓ cup mayonnaise
1 tablespoon Dijon mustard
1 tablespoon Worcestershire sauce
1 to 2 teaspoons Tabasco
⅛ teaspoon freshly ground black pepper
12 finger rolls or white or whole wheat bread
   sliced into circles with a cookie cutter
1 cup alfalfa sprouts, optional

❶ Pulse ham in a food processor. In a medium bowl, combine with relish, mayo, mustard, Worcestershire, Tabasco, and pepper. Mix until well blended.

❷ Spoon filling into bread. Top with alfalfa sprouts, if desired. Makes about 1 dozen finger sandwiches or 4 full sandwiches

Doughnut Sandwich

Doughnut Sandwich
Not for the faint of heart

Americans' love for doughnuts runs deep and dates back centuries: Pilgrims arriving on North America's northeastern coast made these deep-fried sweet cakes in the early 1600s. Today, behemoth chains like Dunkin' Donuts and Krispy Kreme hawk every doughnut imaginable, as do thousands of mom-and-pop shops scattered across North America. Recently, a daring doughnut confection surfaced: the Doughnut Sandwich. It exists in many incarnations, but most have a glazed-doughnut base. The doughnut breakfast sandwich is usually filled with eggs and bacon or ham; the doughnut chicken sandwich is made with a fried chicken patty; the doughnut burger takes your standard burger, with toppings included, and stuffs it inside a doughnut. There are even doughnut ice-cream sandwiches. Although the concession stand at the St. Louis Grizzlies baseball stadium began selling doughnut burgers in 2006—a bacon cheeseburger stuffed inside of a Krispy Kreme glazed doughnut—it was Paula Deen who ignited a brouhaha in 2008 with her "Lady's Brunch Burger," a bacon-and-fried-egg-topped burger on a glazed doughnut. Fans and foes alike appeared simultaneously attracted to and repulsed by the unusual combination of ingredients.

---

1 teaspoon fruit preserves, such as raspberry, or 1 teaspoon spicy mustard

1 glazed doughnut, halved lengthwise

2 slices deli ham

1 slice American or Swiss cheese

Spread fruit preserves or mustard inside doughnut. Add ham and cheese. Close sandwich and enjoy. Makes 1

Who Needs Bread When You Have Glazed Doughnuts?

- Frosty Doughnut Sandwich: Spread softened vanilla or chocolate ice cream on a coconut doughnut.
- Doughnut Breakfast Sandwich: Fill a chocolate-glazed doughnut with a scoop of coffee ice cream.

- Double-Decker Doughnuts: Serve filled with burgers, bacon, eggs, and other savory ingredients—at your own risk!

Egg Salad Sandwich

A sandwich that never goes out of style

Most basic Egg Salad Sandwiches consist of two toasted slices of white or wheat bread filled with a creamy, piquant salad of chopped hard-boiled eggs, mayonnaise, salt, and spices.

Egg salad is so beloved that it has not one, but two American holidays: National Egg Salad Week, which falls right after Easter Sunday, and National Egg Salad Month, in May. One of the earliest printed recipes for a sandwich made with egg salad appears in *The Original Boston Cooking-School Cook Book*, written in 1896 by Fannie Merritt Farmer. With the introduction of sliced soft white bread in the 1930s, these sandwiches became a brown-bag lunch staple as well as a common item at delis, diners, and cafeterias. It's no surprise they're especially popular after Easter, when many people are looking for ways to use up egg hunt leftovers.

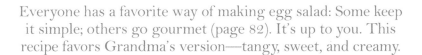

Everyone has a favorite way of making egg salad: Some keep it simple; others go gourmet (page 82). It's up to you. This recipe favors Grandma's version—tangy, sweet, and creamy.

Egg Salad Sandwich

4 eggs
¼ cup mayonnaise
½ teaspoon Dijon mustard
2 teaspoons sweet pickle relish
2 thinly sliced scallions
¼ teaspoon salt
¼ teaspoon freshly ground black pepper
4 slices toasted white, whole wheat, or
    sourdough bread

❶ Place eggs in a large saucepan and fill with enough water to cover by 2 to 3 inches. Bring water to a rolling boil and cook eggs 2 minutes. Remove from heat and let stand 5 minutes. Drain and cool eggs in a bath of cold water for 10 minutes. Peel eggs and let cool to room temperature. In a medium bowl, mash eggs with either a fork or a potato masher.

❷ In a separate small bowl, mix mayo, mustard, relish, scallions, salt, and pepper. Pour over mashed eggs. Stir until combined. Refrigerate at least 3 hours before serving.

❸ Divide egg salad evenly between two slices of toasted bread. Close sandwiches, slice in half on the diagonal, and serve. Makes 2

E
F

Just Add Veggies

- California Egg Salad Sandwich: Add slices of fresh avocado, watercress, and pea shoots and serve on multigrain or sourdough bread.

Gourmet Egg Salad

Consider adding finely chopped fresh vegetables such as celery, red bell peppers, or cucumbers. Or serve with a slice of fresh tomato, a couple lettuce leaves, or a few cooked asparagus spears. Experiment with different spices, herbs, and add-ins: chives, dill, parsley, tarragon, paprika, cayenne, curry powder, mustard seed, capers, horseradish, gherkins, olives.

4 eggs
¼ cup mayonnaise
1 tablespoon Dijon mustard
1 teaspoon lemon juice
2 tablespoons minced shallots
1 finely diced celery stalk with leaves
2 tablespoons finely chopped fresh dill
Several shakes of salt and cranks of freshly ground black pepper

❶ Place eggs in a large saucepan and fill with enough water to cover by 2 to 3 inches. Bring water to a rolling boil and cook eggs 15 minutes. Remove from heat and let stand 5 minutes. Drain and cool eggs under cold running water. Peel eggs and let cool to room temperature. In a medium bowl, mash eggs with a fork or potato masher.

❷ In a separate small bowl, mix mayo, mustard, lemon juice, shallots, celery, dill, salt, and pepper. Pour over mashed eggs. Stir until combined. Refrigerate at least 3 hours before serving. Makes enough for 2 sandwiches

Eggplant Parmesan Sub

An Italian sandwich so hearty you'll forget it's vegetarian

An Eggplant Parmesan Sub consists of a long, crusty loaf split down the center that is packed with several slices of hot eggplant parmigiana smothered in tomato sauce and melted mozzarella or provolone cheese.

The eggplant slices are dipped in egg, then bread crumbs, and either fried or baked until crisp. The cooked eggplant, called eggplant parmigiana, is covered with tomato sauce and a generous amount of mozzarella and grated Parmigiano-Reggiano. Veal and chicken parmigiana are prepared in the same way. Though parmigiana dishes originated in Sicily, they are popular throughout southern Italy. In the United States, you can find Eggplant Parmesan Subs at Italian delis, pizza parlors, and the hundreds of Uncle Tony's or Uncle Vito's joints scattered throughout the country. When ordering one, you can usually just ask for an "eggplant parm."

Making eggplant parmigiana from scratch is time-consuming but simple. It's a good idea to make a double batch to use for leftovers. Refrigerated in an airtight container, eggplant parmigiana will last up to 1 week. San Marzano tomatoes are an Italian plum variety prized for its sweeter, less acidic flavor; they can be found in Italian specialty markets and most major supermarkets. Store-bought tomato sauce can be substituted for the homemade tomato sauce, if you prefer.

Eggplant Parmesan Sub

TOMATO SAUCE

2 teaspoons olive oil

1 shallot, diced

2 garlic cloves, minced

1 (28-ounce) can crushed tomatoes, preferably
San Marzano

¼ teaspoon crushed red pepper flakes

1 teaspoon salt

2 tablespoons fresh basil, finely chopped

2 tablespoons fresh parsley, finely chopped

4 slices baked eggplant (page 86)

¾ cup shredded part-skim mozzarella

½ cup grated Parmigiano-Reggiano

4 to 6 (6-inch) torpedo rolls

❶ Preheat oven to 400°F. In a medium pot over medium heat, warm olive oil. Add shallots and garlic and sauté 2 to 3 minutes, or until translucent. Add tomatoes, red pepper, and salt. Stir until well combined. Reduce heat to medium-low. Let sauce bubble gently 15 to 17 minutes, or until slightly thickened. Remove from heat. Stir in fresh herbs.

❷ To assemble, use either a 9-inch round or 8-inch square baking dish. Cover bottom of dish with a layer of tomato sauce. Add 4 slices baked eggplant (use larger slices on the bottom), and top with one-third of the shredded mozzarella and one-third of the Parmigiano-Reggiano. Repeat two more times until all ingredients are used.

❸ Bake 25 to 30 minutes, or until sauce begins to bubble and cheese turns golden brown. Allow to cool 10 minutes before slicing and layering in crusty rolls. Makes 4 to 6

Baked Eggplant

2 eggs
⅛ teaspoon crushed red pepper flakes
⅛ teaspoon salt
¾ cup bread crumbs (preferably plain)
¼ cup grated Parmigiano-Reggiano
1 large eggplant, cut into ⅜-inch thick slices
Olive oil or non-stick spray

❶ Preheat oven to 400°F. In a small bowl, whisk together eggs, crushed red pepper, and salt. Pour into a wide, shallow bowl or a plate with raised edges.

❷ Place bread crumbs and grated cheese in a separate wide, shallow bowl or plate. Slice eggplant. Dip one slice at a time in egg mixture, allowing excess to drip into bowl, then dredge in bread crumbs, ensuring that entire slice is evenly coated.

❸ Place on a large baking sheet that has been coated with olive oil or nonstick cooking spray. Repeat with remaining slices. Bake eggplant 15 minutes, rotating once, until golden and crisp. Makes 10 to 12 slices

---

Fried Eggplant

2 eggs
⅛ teaspoon crushed red pepper flakes
⅛ teaspoon salt
¾ cup bread crumbs (preferably plain)
¼ cup grated Parmigiano-Reggiano
1 large eggplant, cut into ⅜-inch thick slices
2 to 3 tablespoons extra-virgin olive oil

❶ Prepare eggplant exactly as in steps 1 and 2 above.

❷ Place a large skillet over medium heat. Warm olive oil and fry 4 to 5 eggplant slices at a time. Cook each slice 3 to 4 minutes, turning once, until crisp and golden brown.

❸ Repeat with remaining slices. Drain on a paper-towel-lined plate before assembling in the baking dish. Makes 10 to 12 slices

E
F

The Elvis

Plain old-fashioned mashed banana

He may have been the king of rock and roll, but Elvis Presley had an appetite that was more down-home than aristocratic. A Mississippi boy at heart, Elvis preferred typical Southern favorites, such as buttermilk corn bread, Memphis-style barbecue, banana pudding, and sweet potato pie. His favorite snack, which he apparently taught the cooks at Graceland to make, was his mama's grilled peanut butter, banana, and bacon sandwich. Today the Elvis can be found on the menus of diners and sandwich shops across the United States.

The King allegedly preferred mashed bananas, but slices work just fine. He also liked his peanut butter smooth and creamy and his bacon burnt. Unless you're a truly dedicated Elvis Presley fan, the burnt bacon is optional. True to his Southern roots, Elvis washed down his peanut butter and banana sandwiches with a glass of rich, creamy buttermilk.

---

2 tablespoons peanut butter
2 slices white bread
1 ripe banana, mashed
2 slices cooked bacon
2 tablespoons butter

❶ Spread peanut butter on one slice of bread, banana on the other. Add bacon slices and close sandwich.

❷ Melt butter in a skillet over medium heat. Cook sandwich 2 minutes per side, or until golden. Eat it while it's hot. Keep all the ingredients close at hand—you'll likely be making another. Makes 1

"Back when I was dating him, he liked just a plain old-fashioned mashed banana." Nicknamed "Little" and "Little Bitty" by the King, Anita Wood was Elvis's "No. 1 Girl" in the late 1950s. "He called me little because I was little at the time, tiny. 'Little girl, go fix me a sandwich, peanut butter and jelly sandwich.' Now, you know, back when I fixed a sandwich for him, we mixed up the peanut butter and banana together. We didn't put it in butter and put it in a skillet. We just put it on white bread."

The Elvis

Falafel Pitas

Fast and fresh sandwich pockets

A favorite snack food in Middle Eastern culture, falafel are small fried patties of spiced chickpeas and/or fava beans. They can be served sandwich-style, tucked inside a pita bread and topped with tahini sauce, cucumber yogurt sauce (tzatziki), lettuce, tomato, and onions.

The falafel's origin remains debatable, with many Middle Eastern countries laying claim to it. Most people agree that the first falafel was made from dried fava beans in Egypt and that chickpeas were introduced as the dish spread throughout the neighboring regions. Today, falafel-selling street vendors are ubiquitous in the Middle East, and in America this easy-to-eat dish has stayed true to its street-food roots. It is typically found at inexpensive Middle Eastern and Mediterranean delis, sandwich shops, and food carts.

Prepared tahini (a paste of ground sesame seeds) and tzatziki sauce are found at Middle Eastern specialty markets as well as large supermarkets.

---

4 pieces pita bread or Lebanese flat bread

Prepared tahini, to taste

12 falafel patties (opposite)

Garnishes such as shredded lettuce, diced tomato, and onion slices

1 small container store-bought tzatziki (or homemade, page 157)

❶ Warm pitas. One at a time, coat the inside with a dollop of tahini. Tuck 2 to 3 falafel patties inside.

❷ Add lettuce, tomato, and onion. Drizzle with tzatziki. Serve warm. Makes 3 to 4

Quick and Easy Falafel

Falafel is traditionally made from dried chickpeas that have been soaked overnight. This recipe cuts down on the prep time by using canned chickpeas. (Since these retain more water, a binding agent, such as flour, is needed.)

1 teaspoon olive oil
½ cup diced yellow onion
1 small garlic clove, minced
1 (15-ounce) can chickpeas, drained
¼ cup finely chopped fresh flat-leaf parsley
¼ cup finely chopped fresh cilantro
½ teaspoon ground cumin
¼ teaspoon cayenne pepper
½ teaspoon salt
3 tablespoons all-purpose flour
1 teaspoon baking powder
⅓ cup sesame seeds
¾ cup canola oil for frying

❶ In a small skillet over medium-high heat, warm olive oil. Sauté onions and garlic 3 to 5 minutes, or until soft and golden. Remove from heat.

❷ In a medium bowl, combine chickpeas, parsley, cilantro, cumin, cayenne, and salt. In a small bowl, whisk together flour and baking powder; add to chickpea mixture and stir.

❸ Combine sauteed onions and garlic with chickpea mixture in a food processor. Pulse several times until a paste begins to form. (You should be able to form a patty.) If mixture is dry, add 1 tablespoon water; if wet, add a bit more flour. Transfer mixture to a bowl.

❹ Place sesame seeds in a small, deep bowl. Using lightly floured hands, form falafel mixture into small (2-inch) balls. (It will yield about 12 balls.) Drop each ball one at a time into sesame seeds and coat completely. Gently flatten each ball with the palm of your hand. Place on a cookie sheet lined with parchment or waxed paper.

❺ Pour canola oil into a small, deep pot to a depth of 2 inches and heat over medium heat to 350°F. (Test with a deep-fry thermometer or by dropping a little bit of the falafel into the oil: It should quickly rise to the surface and be surrounded by tiny bubbles.) Fry 1 to 2 patties at a time, avoiding overcrowding, until golden brown and crunchy, about 2 to 3 minutes. Place on a paper-towel-lined plate. Repeat until finished. Makes 10 to 12 patties

E
F

Fish Sandwich

Crispy delcious fish on a bun

A fish fillet sandwich consists of a breaded, deep-fried white fish fillet on a soft bun. Most fast-food Fish Sandwiches come with a slice of cheese and are dressed with mayonnaise or tartar sauce, lettuce, tomato, and pickles.

Americans have been enjoying fried fish fillets since colonial times. After World War II, many restaurants began selling fried fish and chips, from which the fried Fish Sandwich likely evolved. It wasn't until 1962 that the fish fillet sandwich became a staple of American cuisine. That's when Lou Groen created the Filet-O-Fish sandwich for his fledging McDonald's restaurant in Cincinnati, Ohio. Groen's company suffered during Lent, when most Catholics abstain from eating meat; after introducing the Filet-O-Fish, business boomed. Ray Kroc, McDonald's founder, was so impressed that he added it to the McDonald's national menu. Today, more than 300 million Filet-O-Fish sandwiches are consumed each year.

Use a deep fryer if you have one; otherwise, fill a deep, wide, heavy-bottomed pan with enough oil to cover the fish by at least 2 inches. For a lighter alternative, panfry the fish: In a large skillet over medium heat, warm 2 tablespoons olive oil; cook coated fish 3 to 4 minutes per side, or until exterior is golden and crisp.

FRIED FISH FILLETS

1 egg
2 to 3 teaspoons hot sauce
¼ cup all-purpose flour
¼ cup panko or other coarse bread crumbs
¼ teaspoon salt
¼ teaspoon freshly ground black pepper
2 (4-ounce) fillets firm white fish, such as
  tilapia, halibut, or Pacific sea bass
3 to 4 cups canola

About 2 tablespoons butter
2 hamburger buns
¼ cup tartar sauce
2 slices American cheese, optional
Several pickle chips, optional

❶ In a shallow bowl, whisk together egg and hot sauce. Put flour in a separate shallow bowl. In a third shallow bowl, mix bread crumbs with salt and pepper. Pat fish dry with paper towel. Dip each fillet in egg mixture, then in flour; dip again in egg mixture, then dredge in bread crumbs until completely coated.

❷ Pour oil into a deep, wide pan to a depth of 2 inches and heat over medium heat to 350°F. (Use a deep-fry thermometer or test heat by dropping a little bit of batter into oil. It should quickly rise to the surface and be surrounded by tiny bubbles.)

❸ Using tongs, gently place 1 fillet in hot oil. Cook until fish floats and crumbs are golden brown, about 3 minutes. Place fish on a paper-towel-lined plate. Repeat with second fillet.

❹ Butter insides of buns and lightly toast on the stove top or under the broiler. Inside each bun, spread half the tartar sauce and add 1 fillet. Top each with 1 slice American cheese and pickle chips, if desired. Close sandwiches and serve. Makes 2

Serve Fish Sandwiches with a side French fries or
creamy coleslaw and a cold soda.

Fluffernutter

Fluffy peanut-buttery wonderfulness

Possibly the most playfully named sandwich, the Fluffernutter is a beloved New England cousin of the classic **Peanut Butter and Jelly**. Two slices of white bread are held together with creamy peanut butter and a thick layer of sticky, sweet Marshmallow Fluff.

The history of the Fluffernutter is intertwined with that of marshmallow crème, a spreadable concoction of melted marshmallows and corn syrup. In 1913 brother and sister Armory and Emma Curtis opened the Curtis Marshmallow Factory. Their most popular product was Snowflake Marshmallow Crème, which Emma suggested would pair well with peanut butter on a sandwich. So although it appears that Emma Curtis created the sandwich, which later came to be known as a Fluffernutter, its name is actually a registered trademark of Durkee-Mower Inc., the maker of Marshmallow Fluff. Shortly after World War I, Allen Durkee and Fred Mower paid $500 for a marshmallow crème formula created by entrepreneur Archibald Query and christened it "Toot Sweet Marshmallow Fluff." By 1927 it was being sold in retail markets. In the 1930s Durkee-Mower Inc. sponsored a weekly 15-minute radio show called the "Flufferettes." One episode featured *The Yummy Book*—a collection of recipes featuring Marshmallow Fluff—and displayed a photo of the iconic Fluffernutter, which the company describes as a "wonderful concoction of Marshmallow Fluff and peanut butter in a delightfully tasty sandwich!"

---

1 loaf white bread, preferably Wonder
Smooth peanut butter, to taste
Marshmallow Fluff or marshmallow
   crème, to taste

Using one knife, spread one bread slice with desired amount of peanut butter. Using a second knife, spread Marshmallow Fluff. Close sandwich and eat. Makes 1

Fluffernutter Deluxe

- Banana Fluffnutter: Add 1 banana sliced lengthwise, then in half.

- Cinnamon-Sugar Fluffernutter: Sprinkle the gooey filling with lots of sugar (preferably crystallized turbinado sugar) and ground cinnamon.

Fluffernutter

French Dip

French Dip
Meaty goodness dunked in au jus

Accidents can be a blessing in disguise. That's what French emigrant Philippe Mathieu discovered one day in 1918 while working at his Los Angeles sandwich shop, Philippe the Original. Legend has it that as he was making a sandwich for a police-officer patron, he dropped a French roll into some pan drippings. The officer loved the sandwich so much that he returned the next day with several buddies asking for more "dipped" sandwiches. There are three theories to explain why it's called a French Dip: Mathieu was French; the bread was a French roll; the police officer's last name was French. Regardless which is accurate, the French Dip has become the signature sandwich of Los Angeles and is still served daily at Philippe the Original. It consists of a French roll that has been dipped in meat juices and coated in hot mustard and then packed with sliced beef, lamb, pork, turkey, or ham.

MEAT RUB
1 teaspoon dried onion pieces
1 teaspoon dried basil
1 teaspoon dried marjoram
½ teaspoon garlic powder
¼ teaspoon salt
¼ teaspoon black pepper

1 (2- to 2½-pound) rib eye, bottom round,
   or eye of round roast
1 beef bouillon cube, dissolved in 1 cup water
6 French sub rolls, sliced open lengthwise
Hot mustard, optional

❶ Position a rack in center of oven and preheat to 350°F. Combine rub ingredients and using your hands, rub mixture all over meat in a shallow roasting pan. Cook 80 to 90 minutes, or until a meat thermometer reads 140°F for medium rare or 150°F for medium. Remove from oven.

❷ Pour dissolved bouillon in pan. Tent pan with tinfoil and let rest 20 minutes.

❸ Remove meat from pan and place on a carving board. Slice as thinly as possible. Transfer au jus from roasting pan to a shallow saucepan over low heat. Once hot, dip rolls in it (as much as you'd like); spread mustard (if using) inside rolls and fill with meat. Give the sandwiches another dip if you'd like, then eat immediately. Makes 6

Fried Bologna Sandwich

Soft white bread, crispy baloney, and mayo

Though West Virginia introduced the humble Fried Bologna (also spelled baloney) Sandwich, it's become a down-home favorite enjoyed throughout the Midwest, Appalachia, and Hawaii. The sandwich can be found on the menus of diners, mom-and-pop restaurants, and even some ballpark concession stands, namely at the stadium of the Cincinnati Reds. Of course, the best place to get one is in your own kitchen.

If you want to try to make a good thing even better, butter and toast the bread, top the bologna with a slice of American cheese, and add mustard, relish, sweet pickles, or fresh sliced tomato.

---

4 ounces sliced bologna, either one thick steak or several thinner slices

2 slices white bread

1 tablespoon mayonnaise

❶ To prevent ballooning, make a slice in the bologna from the center to the edge. Place it in a hot skillet; no butter or oil is needed, since the meat will release its own fat. Cook until bologna is browned and crisp on the outside yet tender on the inside, about 3 minutes per side.

❷ Spread mayo on both slices of bread. Place hot bologna on bottom slice and close sandwich. Eat it while it's hot. Makes 1

Many purists insist on using only Oscar Mayer sliced bologna. But if you'd like a thicker slice, take a trip to a quality deli, where they can slice it to your specifications.

Fried Bologna Sandwich

Fried Chicken Sandwich

Fried chicken + sandwich = pure genius

A chicken sandwich is a boneless, skinless breast of chicken that is usually breaded and fried or marinated and grilled; otherwise, it's pretty wide open to interpretation. Most fast-food-style chicken sandwiches consist of breaded, deep-fried white meat that is placed on a sesame seed bun and dressed with condiments such as mayonnaise, lettuce, tomato, and pickles. Another version is the **Grilled Chicken Sandwich**, generally consisting of marinated charcoal-grilled white meat served on a toasted bun or artisanal bread, along with condiments ranging from basil pesto to barbecue sauce.

The emergence in the 1920s and '30s of large-scale processing companies such as Perdue and Tyson helped propel the popularity of chicken, whose sliced leftovers quickly became a favorite sandwich filling, notably in the **Classic Club**. In 1967, Truett Cathy, founder of Atlanta-based restaurant chain Chick-fil-A, introduced the Fried Chicken Sandwich: a crispy-on-the-outside, juicy-on-the-inside breaded boneless chicken breast served on a toasted buttered bun alongside dill pickle chips (which Cathy claims was the only condiment he had on hand). Other fast-food chains followed suit. Today chicken sandwiches are ubiquitous, found everywhere from streetside food trucks to high-end restaurants.

Use a deep fryer if you have one; otherwise, simply fill a small, deep, heavy-bottomed pan with at least 3 cups of vegetable or canola oil.

3 to 4 cups vegetable or canola oil

¼ cup all-purpose flour

¼ cup panko or other coarse bread crumbs

2 eggs

1 tablespoon hot sauce

¼ teaspoon garlic powder

2 (4- to 6-ounce) boneless, skinless chicken breasts, pounded with a mallet to about ⅜-inch thick

2 hamburger buns

¼ cup bottled chipotle barbecue or other spicy sauce, divided

2 slices sharp cheddar cheese

4 slices cooked bacon

❶ Set a deep fryer filled with the oil to 350°F, or preheat oil in a small deep pot. Place flour in a small shallow bowl and bread crumbs in another. In a third, whisk together eggs, hot sauce, and garlic powder. Dip chicken first in egg mixture, then flour, then egg mixture again, and finally bread crumbs. This will ensure an extra-thick crunchy coating.

❷ Place chicken in hot oil and cook until golden brown and crispy, about 5 to 7 minutes, flipping once. Place on a paper-towel-lined dish.

❸ Toast hamburger buns in a large skillet over medium heat 2 minutes or until lightly browned. Spread half the barbecue sauce inside each bun; place a piece of cooked chicken on each bottom bun; top each with a slice of cheese and 2 cooked bacon strips; close sandwiches. Eat while hot. Makes 2

E
F

Not All Fried Chicken Comes From Kentucky

- Italian Fried Chicken Sandwiches: Top the fried chicken with sharp provolone cheese and tomato sauce.
- Southern Fried Chicken Sandwiches: Top the fried chicken with pickle chips and creamy coleslaw.

- Spicy Fried Chicken Sandwiches: Top the fried chicken with spicy BBQ sauce, sliced jalapeños, and jalapeño cheese or a smear of pimiento cheese. *Hot!*

Fried Green Tomato BLT

Secret's in the sauce

Of all the variations of a **BLT**, perhaps the most famous is the Fried Green Tomato BLT. An iconic Southern twist on the original, this combination swaps ripe juicy beefsteak tomatoes for tangy unripe green tomatoes, which are dredged in cornmeal and fried until golden and crisp. In addition to the bacon and lettuce, many Fried Green Tomato BLTs are served with herb mayonnaise and melted mozzarella cheese.

Ask most folks and they'll tell you that fried green tomatoes are as richly Southern as collard greens, black-eyed peas, and sweet potato pie. So it may come as a surprise to learn from respected food author and historian Andrew F. Smith that the first published reference to them appeared in an 1835 issue of *New England Farmer*. Whatever their birthplace, these tart fried treats have become a gem of Southern cuisine, one whose popularity grew with the 1991 film *Fried Green Tomatoes*. Today Southern eateries are still the best places to get authentic versions of this regional specialty, served up with charm.

Green tomatoes are available in fall at farmers markets
and roadside vegetable stands, although some supermarkets
carry them. They should be firm and blemish-free.

2 tablespoons mayonnaise

1 tablespoon fresh basil, minced

1 egg

2 to 3 tablespoons whole milk or buttermilk

¼ cup all-purpose flour

¼ cup cornmeal

¼ teaspoon salt

½ teaspoon freshly ground black pepper

1 large green tomato, sliced into ½-inch-thick rounds

½ cup canola oil

4 slices white or wheat berry bread, toasted

4 lettuce leaves

8 cooked bacon slices

❶ In a small bowl, combine mayo and basil; set aside. In a medium bowl, whisk egg and milk; set aside. Place flour in a shallow bowl; in a separate shallow bowl combine cornmeal, salt, and pepper. One at a time, dredge tomato slices in flour, coating both sides, then dip in milk-egg mixture, allowing excess to drip back into the bowl. Coat evenly with cornmeal.

❷ In a small pan, fry tomatoes in canola oil at 350°F until golden brown. Place on a paper-towel-lined plate.

❸ Spread basil mayo on both bread slices. Place lettuce on 2 bread slices and cover each with a tomato slice. Add cooked bacon to both sandwiches and close. Cut sandwiches in half on the diagonal. Y'all make sure to serve your fried green tomato BLT with a tall glass of cold sweet tea. Makes 2

For variety, try adding a few slices of mozzarella or substituting regular bacon with Canadian or applewood-smoked bacon.

Frittata Sandwich
Cheap and easy

Wedges of frittata—an easy-to-make Italian egg omelet—can be served either open-faced or closed on toasted bread. Frittatas are partially cooked in a skillet on the stove top and then baked or broiled in the oven until puffed and golden brown. Popular throughout Italy, they are made differently according to region. Whenever you make them, they're an easy, nourishing, and economical meal. They can be made with virtually any combination of meats, cheeses, and vegetables—even cooked pastas.

The Frittata Sandwich likely evolved as a way to use up leftovers. Commonly home-cooked, they can also be found on the menus of Italian delis and mom-and-pop eateries scattered along the East Coast and in Chicago. Some serve the sandwich on thick slices of focaccia with sliced mozzarella or sharp provolone and a generous ladleful of marinara sauce.

Residents of Malaysia and Singapore enjoy an omelet sandwich known as a Roti John. Minced chicken or mutton, onions, and extra fixings are either fried in an egg omelet and then served on a baguette, or placed inside a hollow roll that's dipped in egg and panfried in its entirety.

Frittata Sandwich

E
F

1 (12-inch) loaf crusty Italian bread, or 2 (6-inch) torpedo rolls, sliced lengthwise but still attached

3 teaspoons olive oil, divided

1 small red-skin potato, diced

1 medium shallot or 1 small yellow onion, thinly sliced

1 small red bell pepper, thinly sliced

5 eggs

1 tablespoon finely chopped fresh basil

1 tablespoon finely chopped fresh parsley

¼ teaspoon crushed red pepper flakes

⅛ teaspoon salt

½ cup grated Parmesan cheese, divided

❶ Drizzle bread with 1 teaspoon olive oil; broil 2 to 3 minutes, or until golden. In a small pot of boiling water, cook potatoes 3 minutes. Drain and set aside.

❷ In a small nonstick skillet over medium-low heat, add remaining 2 teaspoons olive oil. Sauté shallots, peppers, and potatoes 5 minutes, or until golden brown.

❸ Whisk eggs in a small bowl; add herbs, red pepper, salt, and half the Parmesan and gently whisk to combine. Add mixture to skillet. With a fork, gently move it from side to side until eggs start to solidify and a crust begins to form around the edges, 5 to 8 minutes. Jiggle the pan handle and, when eggs are nearly set, remove pan from heat.

❹ Sprinkle frittata with remaining Parmesan and broil 4 to 5 minutes, or until top puffs up and turns golden brown (but doesn't burn). Cool 2 to 3 minutes, slice into wedges, and tuck inside bread. Serve hot or at room temperature with a side of tomato sauce for dunking. Makes 1 (12-inch) sandwich or 2 (6-inch) sandwiches

E
F

Greek Salad Pocket

Easy-to-eat salad with sweet-and-salty creamy dressing

The ever-popular Greek salad may be more American than Greek. An authentic Greek salad, called a country salad (*horiatiki*) in Greece, consists of chopped tomatoes, cucumbers, red onions, kalamata olives, and feta cheese seasoned with olive oil, oregano, basil, salt, and pepper. The Greek salad in America, however, typically includes chopped romaine lettuce and pepperoncini peppers and is usually drowned in a tangy vinegar-based dressing. Nevertheless, the Greek salad is so admired in America that savvy restaurants have begun offering the Greek Salad Pocket, an on-the-go alternative to a traditional fork-and-knife salad. In a pinch, substitute creamy Italian dressing for homemade Greek salad dressing. Hummus can be store-bought or homemade. You can add 1 pound grilled chicken, lamb, or pork to the salad.

GREEK SALAD

2 cups chopped romaine lettuce

¾ cup chopped cucumber

¾ cup cherry tomatoes, halved

⅓ cup kalamata olives, coarsely chopped

1 small red onion, thinly sliced

1 cup crumbled feta cheese

HOMEMADE GREEK SALAD DRESSING

3 tablespoons olive oil

3 tablespoons red wine vinegar

1½ tablespoons lemon juice

¼ teaspoon dried oregano (or 2 tablespoons fresh oregano)

½ teaspoon dried basil (or 6 large leaves fresh basil, thinly sliced)

4 (6-inch) pita pockets

½ cup hummus (page 112)

❶ In a large bowl, toss lettuce, cucumber, tomatoes, olives, onions, and feta cheese. In a small bowl, whisk together all dressing ingredients. Pour on top of salad; toss to coat.

❷ Spread 2 tablespoons hummus inside each pita. Fill with salad and serve at room temperature. Makes 4

Hummus

Making hummus from scratch is quick and easy—not to mention cheap. It adds healthy protein and deliciousness to sandwiches like kofta pockets, paninis, veggie sandwiches, and more. Tahini is a thick paste of ground sesame seeds. It can be found at Middle Eastern specialty markets as well as the ethnic foods section of most major supermarkets.

1 teaspoon olive oil
1 garlic clove, minced
1 scallion, chopped
1 (15-ounce) can chickpeas, drained and
    rinsed
3 tablespoons tahini
3 tablespoons lemon juice
½ teaspoon salt
¼ teaspoon cayenne pepper
¼ teaspoon ground cumin
⅓ cup chopped fresh flat-leaf parsley

❶ Warm oil in a small skillet over medium heat. Add garlic and scallions and sauté until just lightly browned and fragrant.

❷ Transfer to a food processor. Add remaining ingredients and 1 tablespoon water. Process until smooth. Add more water as needed until desired thickness is reached. Makes 1⅓ cups

Grilled Cheese
Crunchy gooey cheesey goodness

The quintessential Grilled Cheese consists of hot, melted American cheese between two crunchy, buttery slices of white toast. It evolved sometime in the 1920s: In 1920 Wonder began selling whole loaves and, in 1930, introduced sliced bread; Kraft Foods sold its first processed canned cheese to the U.S. Army in 1917, and then, to Americans' delight, introduced Velveeta in 1928. (Individually wrapped cheese slices came later, in 1965.) The grilled cheese quickly became a classic—easy to make, inexpensive, filling, and delicious. Entire cookbooks are dedicated to the humble sandwich, and, according to consumer research firm NDP Group, Inc., Americans eat 2.2 billion of these crunchy-gooey sandwiches each year!

About 1 tablespoon butter
2 slices of your favorite soft white bread
2 slices of your favorite American cheese

❶ Butter one side of each slice of bread. Place one slice, buttered side down, and top with both slices of cheese, slightly overlapping them. Top with second slice of bread, buttered side up. Close sandwich.

❷ In a preheated nonstick skillet, grill sandwich 2 minutes, or until underside is golden brown and cheese has begun to melt. Flip with a spatula and press lightly to flatten. Cook 1 minute more, or until bread is golden brown and cheese is completely melted. Slice in half on the diagonal. Eat it while it's hot. Makes 1

There's More Than One Way to Make a Grilled Cheese

- Substitute cheddar, Swiss, or Havarti cheese for the American.
- Swap white bread for multigrain or whole wheat.
- Add a slice of fresh tomato, a couple strips of cooked bacon, or a slice of smoked ham.
- Get fancy with an **Artisanal Grilled Cheese**.

Grilled Cheese

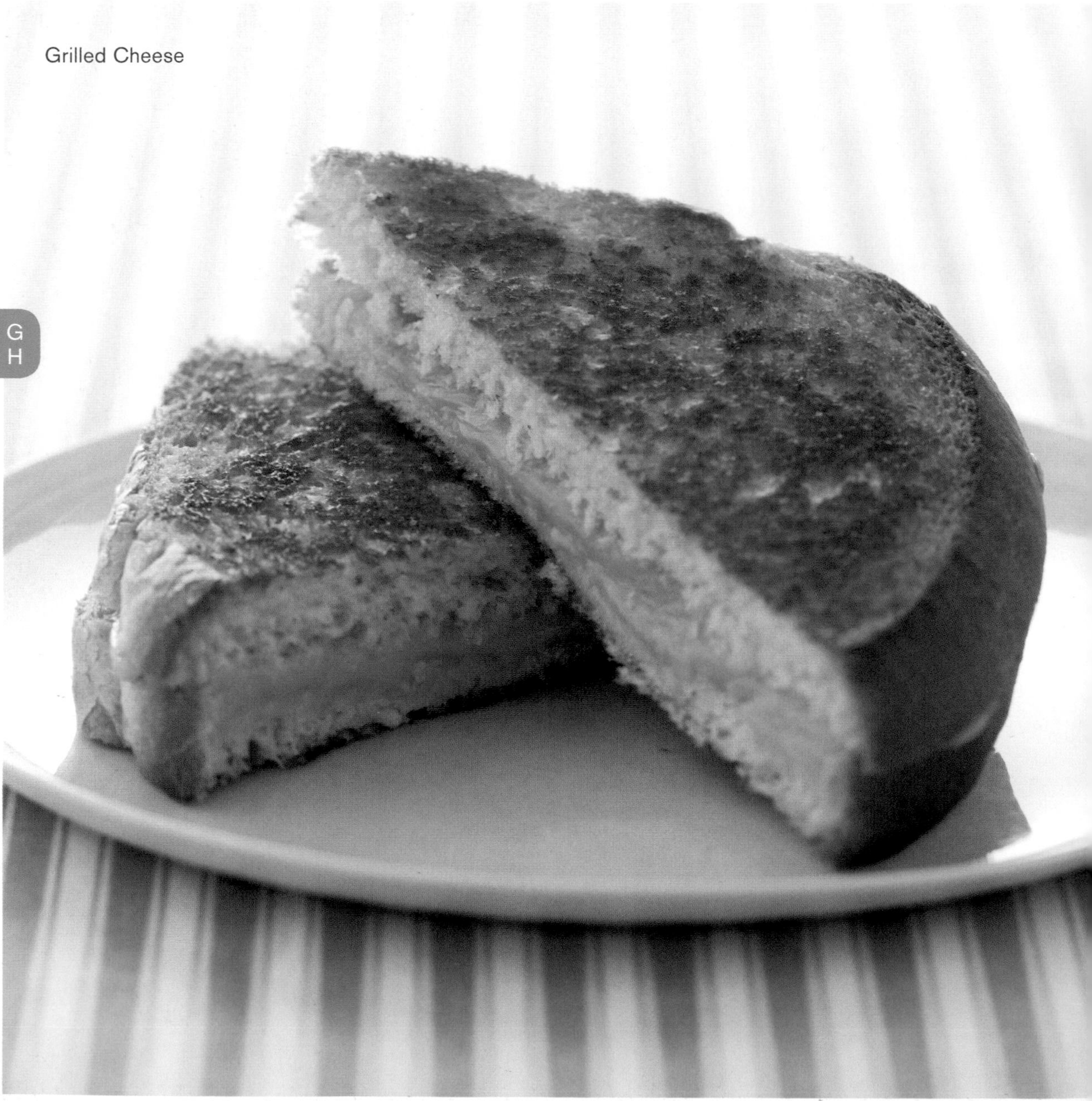

Grilled Chicken Sandwich

Grilled Chicken Sandwich

Lean and mean

This healthy classic starts with a boneless, skinless breast of chicken that is usually marinated, then grilled. It's served on either a toasted bun or artisanal bread and includes any number of garnishes and condiments, ranging from American cheese and pickles to fresh buffalo mozzarella and olive tapenade.

The Grilled Chicken Sandwich evolved in the late 1980s and early '90s as a healthier alternative to breaded fried sandwiches. Today, virtually every fast-food chain offers their own version, and it's a staple menu item at most casual restaurants and bistros. They can be simple or chic and are easily made into an ideal alfresco meal during the summer months.

Serve with a glass of chilled white wine and a side salad
for a fuss-free summer dinner.

GRILLED CHICKEN

2 (4- to 6-ounce) boneless, skinless chicken breasts

1 tablespoon olive oil

⅛ teaspoon salt

⅛ teaspoon freshly ground black pepper

SUN-DRIED TOMATO MAYO

¼ cup mayonnaise

2 tablespoons diced sun-dried tomatoes

1 small loaf focaccia, cut into 2 large squares, each split in half

4 slices smoked mozzarella

4 marinated artichoke hearts, thinly sliced

¼ cup arugula or mesclun

❶ Preheat grill to medium-high. Brush chicken breasts with olive oil and season with salt and pepper. Grill chicken until cooked through but still tender, 5 to 7 minutes per side. Cool 2 to 3 minutes, then slice on the diagonal into ½-inch-thick pieces.

❷ In a small bowl, mix mayo and sun-dried tomatoes to combine. Spread on insides of focaccia.

❸ Arrange smoked mozzarella and grilled chicken on top, then garnish with artichokes and greens. Serve immediately. Makes 2

G
H

Crispy, Spicy, Bacon-y Variations

- Buffalo Chicken Sandwich: Like the famed wings, but without as many napkins. Dress sliced grilled chicken with tangy barbecue sauce, American or cheddar cheese, lettuce, tomato, and cooling blue cheese dressing.
- Buffalo Mozzarella Grilled Chicken Sandwich: Spread basil pesto and mayonnaise on the bread and then top chicken with fresh buffalo mozzarella, tomato slices, and mesclun.
- California Grilled Chicken Sandwich: Top grilled chicken with honey poppy-seed dressing, crumbled goat cheese, and

mesclun. Serve on sourdough or multigrain.
- Italian Grilled Chicken Sandwich: Spread olive tapenade on focaccia or ciabatta and top with grilled chicken, provolone, and roasted red peppers.
- Tex-Mex Grilled Chicken Sandwich: Top grilled chicken with spicy barbecue sauce, cheddar cheese, avocado slices, and bacon strips. Serve on Texas toast.

Grilled Portobello Sandwich

A mouthwatering vegetarian classic

This vegetarian favorite consists of a marinated, grilled portobello mushroom cap served between two slices of bread and dressed with condiments such as basil mayonnaise and Italian vinaigrette. A Grilled Portobello Sandwich is an offshoot of the grilled portobello burger, which surfaced in the 1990s as a healthy vegetarian alternative to the **Hamburger**. Thanks to the mushroom's unusually meaty texture, these sandwiches are sometimes referred to as vegetarian steak sandwiches. However, some carnivores still think of them as hamburger wannabes.

Gently wash the portobello and remove the stem before marinating. Pair with a mesclun salad and a glass of your favorite wine for a tasty, healthful dinner.

---

1 portobello mushroom cap
1 teaspoon olive oil
2 teaspoons balsamic vinegar
1 teaspoon Dijon mustard
Pinch crushed red pepper flakes
1 tablespoon mayonnaise
2 basil leaves, finely chopped
2 slices focaccia or ciabatta bread
1 (1-ounce) slice fresh mozzarella cheese
1 slice jarred roasted red pepper

❶ In a plastic baggie or airtight container, combine portobello, oil, vinegar, mustard, and red pepper flakes; marinate at least 15 minutes and up to 1 hour.

❷ Preheat grill to medium heat. In a small bowl, stir mayo and basil to combine; set aside. Grill portobello 3 to 4 minutes per side, or until lightly charred and tender.

❸ Spread basil mayo on the insides of both slices of bread. Place grilled portobello on bottom half. Top with mozzarella and roasted red pepper. Serve immediately. Makes 1

Grinder

A hardworking sandwich

A Grinder is made from a crusty Italian loaf split lengthwise and filled with various Italian cured meats and cheese, typically provolone. It is dressed with lettuce, tomatoes, onions, and condiments such as mayonnaise and Italian dressing and can be served either cold or hot.

Though the exact origin of this macho sandwich is unclear, most agree that it was created by Italian immigrants in the northeastern United States at the turn of the twentieth century. During World War I, Italian immigrants set up pushcarts and sandwich shops near the shipyards; there they made oversized hearty sandwiches filled with various meats and cheeses for the workers. Many immigrants referred to these hardworking men as "grinders," and eventually the name stuck for the sandwich, too. Grinder is a regional name for the sandwich; depending on where you live, it could be called a **Submarine Sandwich**, **Hoagie**, **Hero**, torpedo, or bomber.

---

1 (12-inch) crusty roll, sliced lengthwise

2 tablespoons mayonnaise

4 thin slices mortadella

4 thin slices Genoa salami

4 thin slices prosciutto, domestic or imported

4 thin slices sharp provolone cheese

4 thick slices tomato

½ cup red onion, sliced paper thin

1 cup shredded lettuce

3 tablespoons Italian dressing or a mixture of olive oil and red wine vinegar

❶ Place split roll on a cutting board. Spread mayo on each half. On the bottom, layer slices of mortadella, salami, prosciutto, and provolone. Add tomatoes, onions, and lettuce and drizzle with dressing.

❷ Close sandwich. Slice in half before serving. Makes 1

Though the Italian dressing is usually drizzled over the fillings, you can also pour some directly onto the bread so it soaks up the flavor.

G
H

Ham and Cheese Sandwich

The quintessential American brown-bag lunch

A Ham and Cheese Sandwich, casually called "ham and cheese," consists of sliced boiled or baked ham, sliced cheese (usually Swiss, American, or cheddar), and condiments such as lettuce, tomato, mayonnaise, and mustard, all served neatly on two slices of untoasted white bread.

No one person is credited with its invention, though it likely evolved as a way to make a basic **Ham Sandwich** more flavorful and filling. The introduction of soft white bread in the early 1900s greatly increased the popularity of lunch-bag sandwiches like the ham and cheese. They were fast and easy to assemble, traveled well, and delighted schoolchildren and working adults alike—and they remain one of America's favorite lunches, dinners, and anytime snacks. If you see items such as a "dipped" or "French toast" Ham and Cheese Sandwich on a menu, they likely refer to a **Monte Cristo**—a hot version that has been dipped in egg and then sautéed in butter until golden brown.

---

1 tablespoon mayonnaise
2 teaspoons yellow mustard
2 slices white or wheat bread, untoasted
2 slices boiled ham
1 slice Swiss or American cheese
2 iceberg or romaine lettuce leaves
2 thin slices fresh tomato

Spread mayo first, then mustard, on both slices of bread. Place ham on one slice and top with cheese. Add lettuce and tomato slices. Close sandwich and serve. Makes 1

Hamburger

One of the most popular sandwiches on the block

A Hamburger, or burger, is a round, cooked ground-beef patty sandwiched neatly inside a bun and traditionally dressed with mustard, ketchup, lettuce, tomato, onions, and pickles.

Known originally as a hamburger sandwich, the humble hamburger was introduced to America by German immigrants in the mid-nineteenth century. By the early twentieth century, hamburgers were a popular food at fairs and streetside food carts. Yet they took a big hit in 1906 with the publication of *The Jungle*, Upton Sinclair's exposé of the meatpacking industry. In 1921 Billy Ingram and Walter Anderson helped rebrand the hamburger when they opened the White Castle System of Eating Houses, offering diners a 5-cent hamburger. The chain emphasized food safety and cleanliness, helping to convince wary Americans that it was safe to eat hamburgers again. They also introduced the concept of take-out fast food, paving the way for giant franchised burger chains like McDonald's, which opened its doors in 1940. In the 1950s and '60s the hamburger was synonymous with suburban teens and carhops; by the 1970s, McDonald's was king, churning out millions of patties every year. Whether it's a plain-ole patty or a gourmet grass-fed version stuffed with Gorgonzola cheese, the hamburger remains America's favorite sandwich and is considered a symbol of American culture worldwide.

Serve with French fries and a thick frothy milkshake
or an icy cold soda.

4 to 6 ounces ground chuck, at least 85% lean

⅛ teaspoon salt

⅛ teaspoon freshly ground black pepper

1 sesame-seed hamburger bun, halved lengthwise

2 thin slices tomato

2 to 3 lettuce leaves, such as Boston or iceberg

3 to 4 pickle chips

A swirl of ketchup

A swirl of yellow mustard

Optional garnishes and condiments: American cheese, raw onion slices, relish, mayonnaise

❶ Preheat grill to medium. Place meat in a bowl and sprinkle with salt and pepper. Gently form a patty; try not to overwork the meat or it will lose its juiciness. Gently press middle of patty with your fingertips to flatten it like a hockey puck. Grill 3 to 4 minutes; flip once, then cook another 3 to 4 minutes, or until meat reaches the desired level of doneness (140°F for medium-rare and 150°F for medium; the USDA recommends cooking beef to 160°F for maximum safety).

❷ Place hamburger on bun. Top with tomato, lettuce, pickles, ketchup, mustard, and other garnishes of your choice. Makes 1

Burger Deluxe

- Cheeseburger: Top a burger with cheese. The most popular cheeses are white or yellow American or cheddar.
- BBQ-Bacon Burger: Top a hamburger with your favorite barbecue sauce, a couple slices of cooked bacon, and cheddar cheese.
- Bun Kabab: Pakistan's variation—a spicy patty made of beef and egg in a hamburger bun—is sold by street vendors countrywide.
- Chili Cheeseburger: Smother a burger with your favorite chili and cheddar cheese.
- Chimichurri: Popular at snack stands in the Dominican Republic, this beef or pork patty is served with cabbage on a bun.

- Gourmet Burgers: Experiment with grass-fed or expensive types of meat, namely Kobe beef, bison, and buffalo. Fancy toppings can include handcrafted cheeses, organic vegetables, and such unexpected ingredients as wasabi or pancetta.
- Slugburger: This little fried patty—made from a mixture of meat and an inexpensive extender such as soybean grits or potato flour—is named not for the slimy garden-dwelling creature but for a slang term for "nickel," which is what it once cost. It's so beloved in Corinth, Mississippi, that folks there have held an annual Slugburger Festival since 1988.

Veggie Burgers

A meatless patty can be made from any variety of ingredients, such as textured vegetable protein, tofu, legumes, vegetables, nuts, and grains. Like a meat patty, veggie burgers can be grilled, broiled, or cooked on the stove top and garnished with traditional toppings, like onions, tomatoes, lettuce, cheese, and pickles.

BULGUR PATTIES
¼ cup uncooked bulgur
2 tablespoons sliced shallots
½ cup canned chickpeas, drained
⅓ cup coarsely chopped walnuts
⅓ cup chopped white button mushrooms
3 tablespoons chopped flat-leaf parsley
⅛ teaspoon salt
¼ teaspoon crushed red pepper flakes
2 teaspoons spicy mustard
2 teaspoons low-sodium soy sauce

1 tablespoon olive oil
2 kaiser rolls
2 teaspoons mayonnaise or mustard
4 slices tomato
6 slices avocado
2 to 3 tablespoons alfalfa sprouts
Garnishes of your choice, such as salsa,
    onions, radishes, and your favorite cheese

❶ In a small pot over high heat, combine bulgur and ½ cup water. Bring to a boil and cook 2 minutes. Lower heat to a simmer, partially cover, and cook 10 minutes, or until water is absorbed and bulgur is cooked through yet still firm. Let cool.

❷ In a medium bowl, combine cooled bulgur with remaining patty ingredients. Transfer mixture to a food processor and pulse several times until a paste begins to form. Remove mixture from processor and, using your hands, shape into 2 round patties. Place on a parchment-lined baking sheet and refrigerate 15 to 20 minutes.

❸ Warm oil in a large skillet over medium-high heat. Add patties and cook 3 to 4 minutes per side, or until browned. Place each burger on a bun and top with mayo or mustard, 2 tomato slices, 3 avocado slices, alfalfa sprouts, and any other desired garnishes. Makes 2

G
H

Ham Sandwich

Plain and simple

A basic Ham Sandwich is nothing more than good sliced boiled ham on untoasted white bread dressed with a dollop of mustard or mayonnaise. Popular versions include the baked ham sandwich, made from carved slices of (preferably hot) country baked ham dressed with Dijon or sweet mustard; the fried ham sandwich, made with thick slices of baked ham fried in butter and served on buttered toasted bread or biscuits; and the Smithfield ham sandwich, made with Virginia Smithfield ham, which is considered by many to be the superlative baked ham.

Elizabeth Leslie (1787–1858), the woman responsible for introducing sandwiches to America, offered a recipe for a ham sandwich in her 1837 book *Directions for Cookery*. It reads: "Cut some thin slices of bread very neatly, having slightly buttered them; and, if you choose, spread on a very little mustard. Have ready some very thin slices of cold boiled ham, and lay one between two slices of bread. You may either roll them up, or lay them flat on the plates. They are used at supper or at luncheon." Leslie would be proud to know that her recipe is still going strong more than 170 years later.

---

2 teaspoons mustard or mayonnaise
of your choice

2 slices white, wheat, pumpernickel,
or rye bread, untoasted

2 slices boiled ham

Spread mustard or mayo on both slices of bread. Place ham on one slice, close sandwich, and serve. Makes 1

Chipped ham, also known "chip-chop" or "chipped-chopped" ham, is seasoned ham that has been sliced ultrathin; it's a beloved sandwich filler in Pennsylvania, and particularly Pittsburgh.

Hero

You've got to be one to finish one

A Hero is a colossal sandwich consisting of several types of cold cuts, cheese, lettuce, tomato, and onions served on a long, crusty Italian roll. It is typically dressed with olive oil, vinegar, salt, and pepper; however, mayo, mustard, pickles, and pepperoncini (pickled Italian sweet peppers) can be added. Though versions consisting of turkey, American cold cuts, and roast beef can be found, traditional examples are made of Italian deli meats and cheeses, such as mortadella, prosciutto, mozzarella, and provolone. They can be served hot or cold.

This supersized sandwich was introduced to America by Italian shipyard workers during World War I. Renowned American food writer Clementine Paddleford inadvertently christened it when she proclaimed, "You have to be a hero to finish one." Subsequently called a hero by New Yorkers, the sandwich is known throughout North America under different regional names: it's a **Hoagie** in Philadelphia, a **Grinder** in Rhode Island, and a sub (short for **Submarine Sandwich**) in most other parts of the United States.

The variations are endless, ranging from cold and hot meats to vegetarian fillings. Since you have to be a hero to finish one, the only accompaniment it needs is a cold soda or beer to wash it down.

Italian soppressata, prosciutto, and fresh buffalo mozzarella can be found in Italian specialty markets or the deli section of most major supermarkets.

2 teaspoons extra-virgin olive oil

1 teaspoon balsamic vinegar

Salt freshly ground black pepper to taste

1 (6- to 8-inch) Italian or French roll, sliced lengthwise down the middle

2 teaspoons mayonnaise, optional

2 thin slices soppressata

3 thin slices prosciutto, preferably imported from Italy

2 thick slices fresh buffalo mozzarella cheese

⅛ cup yellow onion, chopped finely or sliced paper thin

¼ cup shredded romaine or iceberg lettuce

2 thick slices tomato

2 teaspoons sliced pepperoncini, optional

4 basil leaves

❶ In a small bowl, whisk together oil, vinegar, salt, and pepper; set aside. Spread mayo (if using) inside roll, then drizzle with half the oil–vinegar mixture. Layer soppresatta, prosciutto, and mozzarella inside roll. Add onions, lettuce, tomato, pepperoncini (if using), and basil.

❷ Drizzle with remaining oil–vinegar mixture. Close sandwich and dig in. Makes 1

Hoagie

A seriously oversized sandwich

Food historians and sandwich enthusiasts continue to fiercely debate the origin of the sandwich known in Philadelphia as a Hoagie. Here's what most agree on: It was created by Italian immigrants in Philadelphia sometime between World War I and the Great Depression and was originally called a "hoggie." Why? One story says that on the city's Hog Island, shipyard workers often lunched on huge homemade sandwiches, prompting locals to call them "hoggies"; that eventually turned into "hoagies." Another story holds that Al DePalma coined the name when he opened his sandwich shop in Philadelphia in 1936. He listed "hoggies" on his menu, named for the people who ate the oversized sandwiches. In 1992, the hoagie was named the Official Sandwich of Philadelphia, trumping the city's other favorite: the **Philly Cheesesteak**.

Most Philadelphians swear that the only place to get a real hoagie roll—oversized, crusty on the outside, soft and chewy on the inside—is their hometown. For those in other towns, substitute a 10- to 12-inch Italian or French roll. Pepperoncini can be found in Italian specialty markets as well as the ethnic food section of most major supermarkets. If you don't want to look like a hoggie, share this stuffed sandwich with a friend. It easily feeds two and pairs well with a side salad. If you're going it alone, skip the sides. You'll be glad you did.

Oink, oink! You don't have to be a
hoggie to eat a whole hoagie.

Hoagie

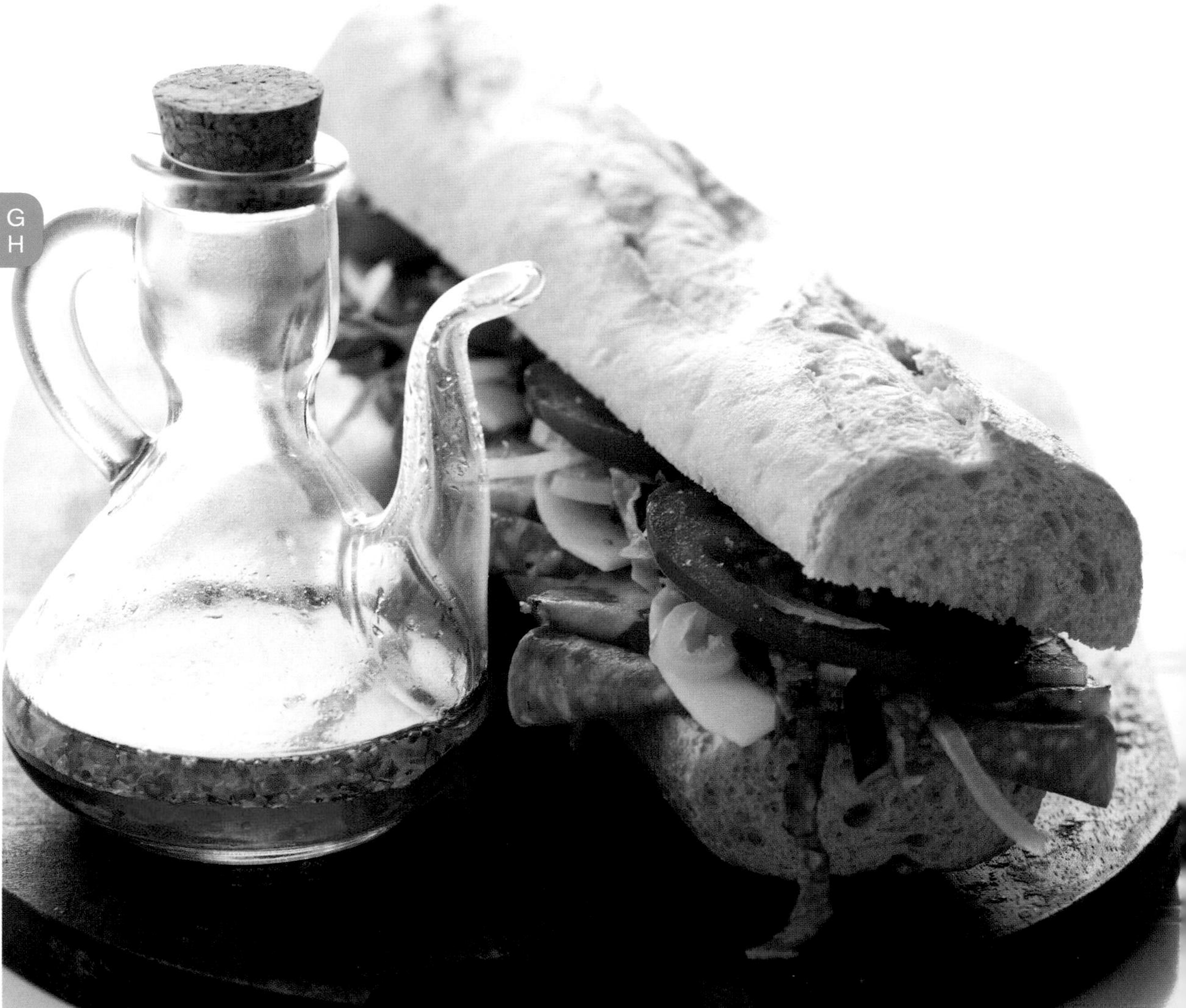

1 tablespoon olive oil

2 teaspoons red wine vinegar

¼ teaspoon crushed dried oregano

Salt and freshly ground black pepper, to taste

1 (10- to 12-inch) Italian or French roll, sliced lengthwise

2 tablespoons mayonnaise, optional

4 thin slices Genoa salami

4 thin slices sweet or hot capicola

4 thin slices sharp provolone cheese

¼ cup yellow onion, chopped finely or sliced paper thin

1 cup shredded romaine or iceberg lettuce

4 thick slices tomato

2 tablespoons sliced pepperoncini

❶ In a small bowl, whisk together oil, vinegar, oregano, salt, and pepper; set aside. Spread mayo (if using) inside roll.

❷ Drizzle with half the oil–vinegar mixture. Layer slices of salami, capicola, and provolone inside roll. Add onions, lettuce, tomato, and pepperoncini.

❸ Drizzle with remaining oil–vinegar mixture. Close sandwich. Slice in half before serving. Makes 1

G
H

Hot Brown Sandwich

This is one sandwich that demands a knife and fork

This open-faced **Turkey Sandwich** with bacon and Mornay sauce is broiled until sizzling. The result is a Hot Brown, a tantalizing combination of textures and flavors: crunchy bread, moist turkey, and crisp bacon, all blanketed in a hot, bubbly cheese sauce. Many also include sliced ham, sliced tomatoes, pimientos, and grated Parmesan cheese.

When most Americans hear the word *Kentucky*, they think of the Kentucky Derby—unless they've eaten a hot brown, Kentucky's signature sandwich. It all started in 1923 with a chef named Fred K. Schmidt, who worked at Louisville's Brown Hotel. The hotel's dinner dances drew more than 1,200 people, who, after hours of revelry, craved a midnight snack. Bored with serving prosaic ham and eggs, Schmidt created this tasty open-faced sandwich. It was an instant sensation and quickly led to many variations such as ham and chicken hot browns, cheddar cheese hot browns, and even vegetarian hot browns made with avocado and tofu—though they bear little resemblance to the real thing.

You can find the hot brown at eateries throughout Kentucky and bordering states, but the best place to eat one is still the Brown Hotel. The following recipe is reprinted with the hotel's permission. Though some establishments substitute cheese for the Mornay, stick with the sauce for an authentic experience.

Cover turkey and bacon in gooey melted cheese sauce,
and you've the perfect after-party midnight snack.

½ cup (1 stick) butter
About 6 tablespoons flour
3 to 3½ cups milk
6 tablespoons grated Parmesan cheese,
  plus extra for topping
1 egg, beaten
About 2 tablespoons whipped cream
Salt and pepper, to taste
8 to 12 slices toast
8 to 12 slices roast turkey
8 to 12 strips cooked bacon

❶ Preheat broiler. In a saucepan over medium-low heat, melt butter. Whisk in flour until all the butter is absorbed, making a thick roux. Add milk and Parmesan cheese. Stir in egg to thicken, but do not allow sauce to boil. Remove from heat. Fold in whipped cream. Add salt and pepper to taste.

❷ For each sandwich, place 2 slices of toast on a metal (or flameproof) dish. Top with a liberal amount of turkey. Pour a generous amount of sauce over turkey and toast. Sprinkle with additional Parmesan cheese.

❸ Place dish under broiler until sauce is speckled brown and bubbly. Remove from broiler, cross 2 strips bacon on top of each sandwich, and serve immediately. Makes 4 to 6

Crust removal is traditional but optional—as is the dollop
of whipped cream in the Mornay sauce.

Hot Dog
The classic frankfurter sandwich

Many wouldn't call this little sausage tucked between bread a sandwich, but in its early days it was indeed called a "frankfurter sandwich." Whether it's called a frankfurter, frank, wiener, wienie, dog, or red hot, a Hot Dog is one of America's quintessential fun foods, associated with baseball games, amusement parks, and campfires. As the names "frankfurter" and "wiener" suggest, hot dogs were introduced to America in the nineteenth century by central European immigrants who sold them from food carts. By the 1920s hot-dog stands were popping up all over the country, the most celebrated being Nathan's Famous on Coney Island, New York, founded in 1916 by Polish immigrant Nathan Handwerker. Many cities and baseball stadiums boast signature varieties, such as the Chicago-Style hot dog or the Fenway Frank at Boston's eponymous ballpark.

G
H

1 hot dog of your choice
1 hot dog bun, preferably top-split
Your favorite condiments

Preheat grill to medium-high. Grill hot dog until evenly and lightly charred, about 8 to 10 minutes. Place in bun and dress with condiments as desired. Makes 1

To steam hot dogs, bring water to a boil, reduce heat to low, and place hot dog in steamer basket. Cover and cook until heated through, 6 to 7 minutes.

Hot Dog

G
H

The United States of Hot Dogs

- Chicago-Style: Grill an all-beef frank and place on a poppy-seed hot dog bun. Top with relish, yellow mustard, tomato wedges, pickle spears, chopped onions, celery salt, and sport peppers (small, mildly hot green peppers), if desired. This variation never includes ketchup.
- Coney-Style (Midwest): Grill or steam a small all-beef hot dog and place inside a steamed bun. Top with minced meat chili, mustard, and chopped onions; a "loaded" dog comes with shredded cheddar cheese.
- Foot Long (North America): Twelve inches of deliciousness.
- Kansas City–Style: Grill hot dog and top with Swiss cheese and sauerkraut.
- Mother-in-Law (Chicago): Sandwich a corn tamale and chili instead of a frankfurter inside a hot dog bun.
- New York System Hot Wieners (Rhode Island): Cook all-beef hot dogs on a griddle and smother with mustard, chopped onion, meat sauce, and celery salt.
- Seattle-Style (Pacific Northwest): Grill a hot dog and top with cream cheese and diced scallions.
- Sonora Dog (American Southwest): Wrap a hot dog in bacon and top with tomatoes, onions, mayo, ketchup, mustard, beans, salsa, and cheese. It's usually served with a roasted chili on the side.
- Texas Wieners (New Jersey): Grill or deep-fry hot dogs and top with spicy brown mustard, chopped onions, and meat sauce.

Making hot dogs is highly subjective. A two-in-one contraption known as the hot dog toaster is now on the market; however, grilling and steaming are the methods of choice. Garnished with mustard, ketchup, relish, mayo, onions, or chili, dogs can be kosher, chicken, turkey, or soy.

G
H

Hot Roast Beef
An oversized plate of comfort

This is not merely a cold **Roast Beef Sandwich** that is served warm; rather, this specialty is sandwich of hot roast beef served open-faced on thick white bread with a scoop of fluffy mashed potatoes and a hot drizzle of rich brown gravy.

The hot Roast Beef sandwich has long been a friend of the economical home cook, for it's an easy way to use leftover meat and bread. It is particularly popular in the Midwestern United States and is known by several different regional names. You can find these gut-busters at community suppers as well as on the menus of diners, old-time lunch counters, and cafeterias. If you're planning a trip to Mount Rushmore, in South Dakota, be sure to drive about 1½ hours northeast to the small town of Wall, where you'll find the billboard-famous Wall Drug Store, in business since 1931. According to Becky Mercuri of *American Sandwich*, this fun kitsch-filled pit stop is one of the very best places to indulge in an authentic Hot Roast Beef.

ROAST BEEF
1 teaspoon dried onion pieces
1 teaspoon dried basil
1 teaspoon dried marjoram
1/2 teaspoon garlic powder
1/4 teaspoon salt
1/4 teaspoon black pepper
1 (2- to 2 1/2-pound) rib eye, bottom round, or
    eye of round roast

8 to 12 slices thick-cut white bread, such as
    Texas toast, toasted or untoasted
About 3 cups mashed potatoes
About 1 cup gravy

❶ Preheat oven to to 350°F.

❷ In a small bowl, combine spices, salt, and pepper. Using your hands, rub mixture all over meat. Place in a shallow roasting pan. Cook 80 to 90 minutes, or until a meat thermometer reads 140°F for medium rare or 150°F for medium.

❸ Remove pan from oven. Tent with tinfoil and let meat rest 20 minutes. Remove meat from pan and slice as thinly as possible. Reserve pan juices for gravy.

❹ Top two bread slices with a scoop of mashed potatoes and some roast beef. Drown it all with gravy. Repeat. Makes 4 big or 6 average sandwiches.

Easy Homemade Mashed Potatoes

2 ½ to 3 pounds potatoes (preferably Yukon
　　Gold), peeled and diced
¼ cup (1/2 stick) butter
¼ cup milk or half-and-half
¼ teaspoon salt
¼ teaspoon freshly ground black pepper

❶ Place potatoes in a large pot or saucepan
and cover with cold water. Bring to a boil, then
lower heat, cover, and cook 12 to 15 minutes,
or until tender. Drain.

❷ Transfer potatoes to a large bowl, and add
remaining ingredients. Puree in a food processor or beat with an electric mixer until smooth.

Gravy

2 to 3 tablespoons pan drippings
2 tablespoons cornstarch
2 cups beef broth, warmed
¼ teaspoon freshly ground black pepper
Several drops Kitchen Bouquet, optional

❶ In a small pot over high heat, add pan
drippings.

❷ Dissolve cornstarch in warm broth until no
clumps remain. Pour into pot. While whisking
mixture, bring to a boil. Reduce heat and simmer 5 minutes or to desired consistency is
reached. Stir in black pepper and a few drops
of Kitchen Bouquet, if using.

G
H

Hot Roast Beef

Ice Cream Sandwich
Sweet 'n' frosty treats

Some of the first Ice Cream Sandwiches were slabs of vanilla ice cream sandwiched between two wafers sold from New York City street vendors at the turn of the twentieth century. They were initially marketed as a quick, refreshing way to beat the city's summer heat, and everyone from kids to businesspeople was instantly hooked. They gained a wider following with the emergence of ice cream trucks in the 1920s, becoming a staple in many American freezers by the 1950s and '60s thanks to their availability in supermarkets.

In the 1980s Ray LaMotta invented the Chipwich—two chocolate chip cookies filled with vanilla ice cream and rolled in chocolate chips—helping to make the ice-cream-based sandwich an iconic frozen dessert. Today the chilly treats come in many forms and are making a splash at hip bakeries and ice cream and gelato shops worldwide.

---

2 scoops vanilla ice cream
2 chocolate chip cookies
About ¼ cup mini chocolate chips, optional

❶ Let ice cream rest for a few minutes at room temperature until softened. Spread a thick layer of ice cream on the underside of one cookie.

❷ Top with second cookie, then gently press sandwich closed. If desired, roll edges in mini chocolate chips. Eat immediately or wrap tightly with plastic wrap and freeze in an airtight container up to 3 days. Makes 1

Soften ice cream to a spreadable consistency
so your cookies won't crumble.

We All Scream for Ice Cream Sammies!

- Berry Chocolate Sandwiches: Fill two chocolate or chocolate chip cookies with strawberry or black raspberry ice cream, then roll in chocolate sprinkles.
- Butter Pecan Sandwiches: Fill two vanilla or coconut cookies with butter pecan ice cream, then roll in crushed pecans.
- Ginger Toffee Sandwiches: Fill two ginger cookies with vanilla ice cream, then roll in crushed toffee candy, such as a Heath Bar.

- Mint Chocolate Chip Sandwiches: Fill two chocolate cookies with mint chocolate chip ice cream, then roll in mini chocolate chips or chocolate sprinkles.
- Oatmeal Walnut Sandwiches: Fill two oatmeal cookies with vanilla ice cream, then roll in sweetened coconut flakes or walnuts.

Mix 'n' Match! (and Roll)

Cookies	Ice Cream	Extras
Chocolate	Strawberry	Mini chocolate chips
Chocolate chip	Black raspberry	Chocolate or rainbow
Vanilla	Butter pecan	sprinkles
Coconut	Mint chocolate chip	Crushed walnuts or pecans
Gingersnaps	Cinnamon	Toffee pieces
Oatmeal	Gelato	Shredded coconut
Snickerdoodle	Sherbet	

Making ice cream sandwiches with either homemade
or store-bought cookies is fun and easy. Try rolling them
in decorative candy sprinkles, mini chocolate chips,
crushed candy bars or other extras.

Italian Beef

Juicy seasoned beef and peppers on a fresh sub roll

An Italian Beef is constructed with a long sub roll split down the middle and packed with slices of seasoned cooked beef and topped with *giardiniera* (an Italian relish of pickled vegetables) or Italian sweet peppers and beef juices.

Despite its name, this sandwich originated not in Italy but in Chicago, Illinois. Al's No. 1 Italian Beef opened its first stand in 1938, offering diners an inexpensive, hearty sandwich. Soon similar stands began popping up all over the city, while home cooks made huge batches of the stuff for large Italian weddings, funerals, and parties. Like a **French Dip**, the Italian Beef is dipped in the meat's juices until the bread is wet. When ordering one, you can usually request the degree, from "wet" (just moist) to "soaked" (soggy). Most Chicago Italian beef stands also offer a "combo," which includes cooked Italian sausage along with the beef.

Depending on how much time you have, you can either roast your own meat with the following recipe or simply use high-quality deli roast beef.

MEAT RUB

1 teaspoon dried onion pieces
1 teaspoon dried basil
1 teaspoon dried marjoram
½ teaspoon garlic powder
¼ teaspoon salt
¼ teaspoon black pepper

1 (2- to 2½-pound) rib eye, bottom round,
  or eye of round roast

1 tablespoon olive oil
1 large red bell pepper, cut into strips
1 large green bell pepper, cut into strips
1 beef bouillon cube, dissolved in 1 cup water
6 sub rolls, sliced open
A few spoonfuls giardiniera
Sliced hot peppers

❶ Position a rack in center of oven and preheat to 350°F. In a small bowl, combine rub ingredients. Rub mixture all over meat. Place meat in a shallow roasting pan and cook 80 to 90 minutes, or until a meat thermometer reads 140°F for medium-rare or 150°F for medium.

❷ Meanwhile, add olive oil to a large skillet over medium-high heat. Add peppers and sauté 7 to 10 minutes, or until tender and starting to brown. Set aside.

❸ Remove pan from oven. Pour dissolved bouillon in pan. Tent pan with tinfoil and let rest 20 minutes. Transfer meat to a carving board and slice as thinly as possible. Quickly bathe each slice in au jus and place it onto a roll. Garnish each sandwich with some sautéed peppers, a spoonful of giardiniera, and a few hot pepper slices. Drizzle with a bit more au jus. Serve immediately. Makes 6

Italian Tuna Salad Sandwich

Lose the mayo

An Italian Tuna Salad Sandwich is distinct from a traditional American **Tuna Salad Sandwich** in several ways. It uses imported Italian tuna packed in olive oil but forgoes the mayo. Popular garnishes include celery, olives, capers, and roasted red peppers. And it's served on any crusty Italian bread.

Though tuna packed in olive oil has long been a part of the Mediterranean diet, it has only recently begun to garner serious attention in North America. Imported Italian or Spanish tuna in olive oil is prized for its full-bodied, fresh flavor that is never fishy. Due to their trendy status, you'll likely find Italian tuna sandwiches at fashionable eateries and bistros, although plenty of great Italian American delis and mom-and-pop shops were offering them long before they became chic.

Imported Italian or Spanish tuna packed in olive oil can be found at Italian and Latin groceries and major supermarkets. Bottled tuna is a bit more expensive than canned, and both are more expensive than domestic tuna. If price is a concern, choose domestic tuna packed in olive oil.

Italian Tuna Salad Sandwich

1 (6-ounce) jar or can Italian or Spanish tuna
in olive oil, drained and flaked into chunks
with a fork

1 shallot, minced

⅓ cup diced celery (preferably a pale stalk
with leaves)

¼ cup kalamata olives, pitted and coarsely
chopped

¼ cup sun-dried tomatoes in olive oil,
drained and diced

2 teaspoons capers, drained

2 tablespoons finely chopped fresh parsley

2 tablespoons finely chopped fresh basil

1 tablespoon plus 2 teaspoons extra-virgin
olive oil, divided

1 tablespoon lemon juice

2 teaspoons red wine vinegar

Salt and freshly ground black pepper, to taste

1 (12-inch) crusty baguette, split down the
middle and toasted

¼ cup fresh arugula leaves or mesclun

¼ cup thinly sliced fennel bulb

❶ In a medium bowl, mix tuna, shallots, celery,
olives, sun-dried tomatoes, capers, parsley, and
basil. In a small bowl, whisk together 1 tablespoon of the olive oil, lemon juice, vinegar, salt,
and pepper. Pour over tuna mixture and stir until
well blended.

❷ Brush insides of bread with the remaining
2 teaspoons of olive oil. Broil 2 to 3 minutes,
or until crisp and golden brown.

❸ Place toasted baguette on a clean work surface. Cover bottom half with fennel and greens.
Slice in half. Serve at room temperature. Makes 1

Add-ins include roasted red and yellow peppers, sliced marinated
artichoke hearts, or anchovy fillets. Italian tuna salad can be served
at room temperature or slightly chilled.

Jucy Lucy

As fun to eat as it is to say

When you bite into this "inside-out" **Cheeseburger** (page 128), a surge of gooey cheese flows out from its center. Although everyone agrees that the Jucy Lucy was born in Minneapolis, some credit Matt's Bar with its invention, and others claim it was the brainchild of the 5-8 Club. Matt's motto is, "If it's spelled correctly, you're at the wrong place." No matter where you eat one, remember this caveat: Let the burger cool slightly before biting into it. Overeager Jucy Lucy lovers will tell you that pizza burn's got nothing on the blister that will form on the roof of your mouth from molten-hot oozing cheese.

2 pounds ground chuck, preferably
    85 percent lean
Salt and freshly ground black pepper
6 slices cheese, such as American or cheddar,
    cut into quarters
6 hamburger buns
Garnishes, such as lettuce, tomato, pickle
    slices, and fried onions

❶ Preheat grill to medium. Season meat with salt and pepper. Divide into 12 equal patties, being careful not to overwork meat.

❷ Neatly stack 4 quarter slices of cheese in the center of each patty and top with a second patty. Using your fingertips, seal patties together. (The patty will have a small bump in the middle from the cheese.)

❸ Place patties on grill, with the cheese-bump side up. Cook 6 to 7 minutes, flip, and pierce sides with a knife to let steam from the cheese escape. Cook another 6 to 7 minutes. Remove burgers from grill. Serve on buns and top with your choice of garnishes. Let cool slightly before eating. Makes 6

Kofta Pockets
Pitas stuffed with tasty char-grilled meatballs

According to *The Oxford Companion to Food*, "the word *kofta* is derived from the Persian *koofteh*, meaning 'pounded meat.'" In English the term is used to describe several types of meatballs that are prevalent in Middle Eastern, Indian, Asian, Balkan, and North African cuisines. Ingredients, cooking methods, and serving suggestions vary widely according to regional cuisines.

In America, the Kofta Pocket typically begins with ground lamb or beef that is mixed with ingredients like rice or bulgur wheat, onions, and spices; the mixture is formed into meatalls that are char-grilled, nestled inside a warm pita, and covered with such toppings as yogurt sauce, hummus, onions, tomatoes, and lettuce. Vegetarian kofta is made from paneer (a soft Indian cheese) or vegetables.

Broil kofta for 8 to 10 minutes, rotating skewers, or until the meat is evenly browned and cooked through. Alternatively, bake at 350°F, flipping once, for 20 to 25 minutes, or until the meat is evenly browned and cooked through. Or, place 2 tablespoons olive oil in a large skillet over medium-high heat and cook kofta 7 to 10 minutes, turning occasionally, until meat is evenly browned and cooked through.

---

14 to 16 kofta (opposite)
4 pitas, sliced in half and warmed
Tzatziki sauce, to taste (opposite)

Place 2 kofta inside each half pocket; top with a dollop of tzatziki and any garnishes you desire. Eat immediately. Makes 4

Top kofta pockets with thinly sliced red onions, shredded carrots, and baby lettuce leaves.

Kofta

Prepared kofta can be found at specialty ethnic markets. Although kofta are traditionally grilled on skewers, they can also be broiled, baked, or panfried. In the following recipe, pine nuts are ground into a meal as a quick alternative to cooking bulgur from scratch.

1 pound ground lamb (or beef)
2 teaspoons salt
¼ cup minced yellow onion
2 garlic cloves, peeled and smashed
¼ cup fresh parsley, minced
2 teaspoons ground coriander
1 teaspoon ground cumin
½ teaspoon ground cinnamon
¼ teaspoon ground nutmeg
¼ teaspoon cayenne pepper
½ cup toasted pine nuts, ground into a meal
    in a food processor

❶ In a medium bowl, combine all ingredients. Using your hands, mix well until smooth. Refrigerate at least 15 minutes and as long overnight.

❷ When ready to cook, form lamb mixture into 1½ to 2 inch balls. Preheat grill to medium. If using wooden skewers, soak in water for 30 minutes prior to using. Place 4 kofta on each skewer.

❸ Grill, occasionally rotating skewers, 8 to 10 minutes, or until lamb is evenly browned and cooked through. Slide kofta off skewers. Makes about 14 to 16 kofta

K
L

Tzatziki (Cucumber Yogurt Sauce)

1 cup plain Greek-style or regular yogurt,
    strained until thick
½ cup peeled, diced, and seeded cucumber
1 teaspoon lemon juice
1 teaspoon salt
¼ teaspoon sugar
¼ teaspoon cayenne pepper
3 tablespoons minced fresh mint

Combine all ingredients in a small bowl; cover and refrigerate until ready to use.

Kofta Pockets

K
L

Liverwurst Sandwich

Liverwurst Sandwich

A tragically underrated snack

Perhaps the most unfortunately named of all sandwich fillers, liverwurst (from the German *leberwurst*) has endured its share of snarky remarks. A sausage usually made from ground pork, it has a uniquely strong, spicy flavor. Only 10 to 20 percent of the sausage is actually pork liver; other ingredients include pork meat, fat, and spices. In the United States, liverwurst is usually sliced, although spreadable versions can be found.

The American Liverwurst Sandwich often shows its German heritage: It's typically made with rye or pumpernickel bread, spicy mustard, raw onions, sauerkraut, and Swiss cheese. The two best places to get one are a good deli and your own kitchen.

Butter for bread
2 slices dark rye bread
1 tablespoon spicy mustard
2 thick slices (about 3 to 4 ounces) liverwurst
4 thin slices yellow onion
¼ cup sauerkraut, drained of excess liquid

❶ Butter and toast bread. Spread mustard on both slices.

❷ Top one slice with sliced liverwurst, onions, and sauerkraut. Close sandwich and serve.
Makes 1

You can substitute creamy coleslaw for the sauerkraut or add 2 slices of Swiss cheese.

Lobster Roll
Hot or cold, it's total perfection

A Lobster Roll consists of a buttered, toasted hot dog bun that is generously filled with either a cold lobster-salad mixture or hot chunks of lobster liberally drizzled with melted butter.

It's ironic that lobster, one of the world's most luxurious foods, is also the featured ingredient in this, one of New England's least pretentious sandwiches. Its inventor is still contested, but most food historians agree this sandwich is a twentieth-century East Coast creation. According to Jane and Michael Stern of *Roadfood Sandwiches*, when it comes to lobster rolls there are two contending camps: hot vs. cold. The cold lobster roll consists of a lobster salad made with mayonnaise, celery, and seasonings that is placed inside a buttered, toasted hot dog bun. It's the signature Maine version found everywhere from fine dining establishments to seaside shacks. The hot lobster roll, which was created in 1929 by Harry Perry of Milford, Connecticut, is considered by some to be the purebred of the two: Chunks of freshly cooked lobster meat are carefully tucked inside a hot, buttered hot dog bun and doused with melted butter.

Lobster Rolls are best enjoyed with good company, cold beer, and lots of pickles and potato chips on the side, so invite a bunch of friends over. You do the cooking; they'll do the assembling. Skip the china and silverware, but double up on the paper plates and napkins.

K
L

In general, a 1-pound lobster will yield approximately ⅔ cup of meat. A 1½-pound lobster will yield approximately 1⅓ cups of meat.

Lobster Roll

K
L

Cold Lobster Rolls

2½ cups lobster meat, cut into chunks
¼ to ⅓ cup mayonnaise
1 tablespoon lemon juice
⅓ cup finely chopped celery
2 scallions, finely chopped
Salt and freshly ground black pepper, to taste
A few dashes hot sauce, optional
4 tablespoons butter
4 split-top hot dog buns
½ cup shredded lettuce
4 lemon wedges

❶ In a medium bowl, mix lobster, mayo, lemon juice, celery, scallions, salt, pepper, and hot sauce (if using). Stir until well blended. Place in an airtight container and refrigerate at least 30 minutes and up to 2 hours.

❷ When ready to serve, remove lobster salad from refrigerator. Butter buns inside and out. Place on an indoor grill or in a large skillet over medium heat. Toast until golden brown and crisp all over. Divide lobster salad evenly among buns. Top each with lettuce. Serve immediately, with lemon wedges on the side. Makes 4

Hot Lobster Rolls

4 tablespoons room-temperature butter for buns, plus 1 cup hot melted butter for serving
4 split-top hot dog buns
3 cups warm lobster meat, cut into chunks

❶ Liberally butter buns inside and out. Place on an indoor grill or in a large skillet over medium heat. Toast until golden brown and crisp all over. Divide lobster meat evenly among buns.

❷ Serve immediately with melted butter on the side for drizzling over sandwich. (If you put it on the roll too early, you risk a soggy bun. You need a sturdy bread base to cradle all that luscious lobster.) Makes 4

A split-top hot dog bun looks just like it sounds: It has flat sides and a long split along the top, which makes it ideal for lobster rolls.

Loose Meat Sandwich
The pride and joy of the Midwest

Also known as a Tavern, a Maid-Rite, or a Tastee, this hearty sandwich traditionally consists of either plain or lightly seasoned ground beef that is steamed and served loose on a heated hamburger bun. Though it's usually topped with mustard, ketchup, and pickles, any host of toppings, including cheese and chili, can be added. Think of it as an unformed **Hamburger** or sauceless **Sloppy Joe**.

According to Jane and Michael Stern of *Roadfood Sandwiches*, "Sticklers for historical veracity prefer the term 'Tavern,' because that is what it was called when David Heglin first served it in 1924 at a twenty-five-seat Sioux City restaurant he ran called Ye Old Tavern." Though it still answers to various monikers, the sandwich is beloved throughout the Midwest, due in no small part to Floyd Angell, who in 1926 founded Maid-Rite restaurants, a chain specializing in Loose Meat Sandwiches. Just like the original more than 80 years ago, today's Maid-Rites are made from steamed, lightly seasoned ground beef served on a warm bun.

Don't even think about getting your hands on an original Maid-Rite loose meat recipe. They, along with most Midwest chains and eateries, use a special secret seasoning that is as protected as the Hope Diamond. You can, however, order frozen Maid-Rites online that will be delivered straight to your door. Believe it or not, when you order a Maid-Rite at one of the restaurants, it comes with a spoon—so you can scoop up the meat that invariably falls out of the bun.

When preparing a homemade loose meat recipe, many Midwesterners prefer the taste of meat cooked in a cast iron skillet; if you don't have one, a large frying pan will do.

2 tablespoons vegetable oil
1 pound ground chuck
1 cup finely chopped yellow onion
1 ½ teaspoons salt
¼ teaspoon black pepper
1 tablespoon red wine vinegar
1 tablespoon light brown sugar
4 hamburger buns, warmed
4 slices American cheese, optional
Yellow mustard, to taste
A few sliced pickles

❶ Warm oil in a large frying pan over medium heat. Add beef and, using a wooden spoon, break into small pieces. Add onions, salt, and pepper and sauté until meat is lightly browned. Stir in vinegar and brown sugar. Add enough water to just cover meat. Stirring occasionally, simmer uncovered 15 to 20 minutes, or until water has evaporated completely. (Beef should be moist but not wet.)

❷ Spoon meat onto buns, top with cheese (if using), mustard, and a few pickle slices. Serve immediately, either with or without a spoon.
Makes 4

K
L

Loose Meat Sandwich

Meatball Sub

M
N

Meatball Sub

Forget the spaghetti, meatballs belong in a sub

This brawny specialty consists of a crusty Italian torpedo roll split down the middle and stuffed with cooked meatballs, tomato sauce, and mozzarella or provolone cheese. Sautéed green bell peppers and onions are popular toppings as well.

A meatball is a ball of ground meat that is mixed with ingredients such as bread crumbs, eggs, and herbs. It is hand-rolled and either fried, baked, braised, or steamed. Regional variations exist in countries worldwide. In North America, the Meatball Sub is available nearly everywhere, from pizza shops and delis to stadium concessions and food trucks.

Homemade meatballs and tomato sauce will yield the most authentic flavors, but frozen meatballs and store-bought sauce will work in a pinch. To create a sausage sub, substitute cooked Italian sausage for the meatballs. If you can't decide, add sausage to the meatballs for a meatball and sausage sub.

TOMATO SAUCE
2 teaspoons olive oil
2 shallots, diced
4 garlic cloves, minced
2 (28-ounce) cans crushed tomatoes,
 preferably San Marzano tomatoes
½ teaspoon crushed red pepper flakes
2 teaspoons salt
¼ cup fresh basil, finely chopped
¼ cup fresh parsley, finely chopped

24 cooked meatballs (opposite)
8 crusty Italian rolls, split lengthwise
16 slices (about 1 pound) mozzarella or sharp
 provolone

❶ Warm oil in a medium pot over medium heat. Add shallots and garlic and sauté 2 to 3 minutes, or until translucent. Stir in tomatoes, red pepper, and salt. Reduce heat to medium-low. Let sauce bubble lightly 15 to 17 minutes, or until slightly thickened. Turn off heat. Stir in herbs.

❷ Add meatballs to sauce and warm over medium heat 10 minutes, stirring occasionally.

❸ Preheat broiler. One at a time, add 3 meatballs to a roll. Top with sauce and 2 cheese slices. Place on a large baking sheet and repeat with remaining sandwiches. Broil 2 to 3 minutes or until cheese is melted and bubbly and bread is golden. Eat them while they're hot. Makes 8 sandwiches of 3 meatballs each

Beef and Pork Meatballs

½ pound ground beef
½ pound ground pork
1 cup bread crumbs
⅓ cup grated Parmigiano Reggiano
¼ cup chopped fresh flat-leaf parsley
1 egg, lightly beaten
½ teaspoon salt
½ teaspoon freshly ground black pepper
⅛ cup olive oil
⅛ cup canola oil

❶ Place meats in a large bowl with bread crumbs, cheese, and parsley. In a small bowl, beat egg with salt and pepper; add to meat mixture. Mix ingredients with your hands until everything is moist and meat holds together. If too dry, add a bit of water or another beaten egg. If too moist, add more bread crumbs. Once consistency is right, use your hands to roll mixture into 1½-inch balls.

❷ Place oils in a large skillet over medium heat. Fit as many meatballs in skillet as possible without overcrowding. Cook about 2 to 3 minutes until browned; turn and cook another 2 to 3 minutes, until all sides are evenly browned. Place on a paper-towel-lined plate to absorb excess oil. Repeat with remaining meatballs. Note: Meatballs can also be baked. Preheat oven to 400°F. Shape as above and place them on a tinfoil-lined baking sheet (for easy cleanup). Cook 20 minutes, or until browned. Makes about 24 meatballs

M
N

Meatloaf Sandwich

Leftovers done right

This classic American comfort food requires sliced bread, thick slabs of meatloaf, and mayonnaise, mustard, or ketchup. In diners, it's often served open-faced and accompanied by mashed potatoes and brown gravy.

Surprisingly, homemade meatloaf owes its popularity to technology: Ground beef became affordable after the invention of meat choppers during the industrial revolution, and spoilage was no longer a concern after the invention of ice-cooled railroad cars in the 1880s and home refrigeration in the early 1900s. Why is it called meatloaf? Because the meat is mixed with bread crumbs and formed into a loaf shape or cooked in a loaf pan.

Meatloaf is one of the few foods that truly tastes better the next day. It's even delicious cold, straight from the fridge. Cold meatloaf is standard for this sandwich, but it can be served at room temperature or hot, according to personal preference. Boost the flavor by adding barbecue sauce, grilled onions, and cheddar cheese; crispy bacon slices and melted Monterey Jack; or creamy horseradish sauce, caramelized onions, and melted Swiss cheese. Serve it open-faced by arranging 2 slices of toast on a plate, topping them with 2 slices of hot meatloaf, and smothering everything with sautéed mushrooms and gravy.

---

1 tablespoon whole grain mustard

2 slices Texas toast, country white, or whole wheat bread

About 1 tablespoon ketchup

1 (¾-inch-thick) slice meatloaf

Spread mustard on one slice of bread and ketchup on the other. Place meatloaf slice on one piece of bread. Close sandwich and enjoy.

Makes 1

My Mom's Meatloaf

This tried-and-true recipe is perfect for dinner or day-after meatloaf sandwiches. For a softer top, combine 2 tablespoons each Dijon mustard, Worcestershire sauce, and ketchup, and brush on top of meatloaf before cooking. For a crisper, browner top, omit the sauce.

1 tablespoon canola oil
½ cup diced shallots
1 cup diced red bell pepper
1 cup diced zucchini
½ cup diced white button mushrooms
½ teaspoon salt
½ teaspoon freshly ground black pepper
2 pounds ground beef (Mom uses 85% lean)
2 eggs, lightly beaten
1 tablespoon Worcestershire sauce
1 tablespoon spicy mustard
¼ cup ketchup
¾ cup bread crumbs
2 teaspoons hot sauce, such as Tabasco
1 tablespoon olive oil

❶ Preheat oven to 350°F. Lightly grease a large baking sheet. Warm oil in a large skillet over medium-high heat. Add shallots, peppers, zucchini, and mushrooms. Sauté 5 to 7 minutes, or until lightly browned yet still firm. Add salt and pepper.

❷ In a large bowl, combine vegetables with all remaining ingredients except olive oil; mix with your hands until well combined.

❸ Divide meat into two equal ovals. Place on prepared baking sheet. Rub loaves with oil, sprinkle with salt and pepper, and top with sauce (if desired; see headnote). Bake 50 to 60 minutes, or until browned on top and cooked through. Makes 2 meatloaves, enough for about 8 sandwiches

M
N

Monte Cristo

Crunchy sweet-and-savory perfection

This American version of the **Croque-Monsieur** consists of ham, turkey, or chicken paired with Swiss cheese between two slices of white or challah bread that is then dipped in an egg batter and grilled or fried in butter until golden brown. The crispy, savory result is often dusted with confectioners' sugar and served with a side of red currant jelly.

It's not often that a food owes its popularity to both French cuisine and America's Disneyland, yet such is the case with the Monte Cristo. American cookbooks from the 1930s to the '50s include numerous variations bearing less exotic names, such as the French Toasted Cheese Sandwich and the French Sandwich. Though no single American is credited with its creation, California is considered its home. It first appeared on the menu at Gordon's, a restaurant once located on Wilshire Boulevard in Los Angeles, but got its big break when Disneyland's Blue Bayou Restaurant put it on the menu. Though not widely popular today, the Monte Cristo still holds an old-fashioned charm and can be found on menus of both high-end hotels and mom-and-pop eateries.

Red currant jelly is widely available, but strawberry
or mixed-berry jelly make good substitutes.

Monte Cristo

2 eggs
¼ cup whole milk
¼ teaspoon salt
⅛ teaspoon black pepper
Butter for bread, plus more for frying
4 slices bread (white or egg bread,
    such as challah)
4 slices baked ham
4 slices turkey
4 slices Swiss cheese
Confectioners' sugar, for serving
Red currant jelly, jelly of your choice,
    or sweet mustard, for serving

❶ In a medium bowl, whisk together eggs, milk, salt, and pepper. Butter both sides of each slice of bread. Fold 2 slices each ham, turkey, and Swiss cheese between bread. Close sandwiches.

❷ Melt butter on a griddle or in a large frying pan over medium-high heat (pan should be coated). One at a time, dip each sandwich into egg mixture, allowing excess to drip into bowl. Fry about 3 minutes per side, or until both sides are golden brown, adding butter as necessary.

❸ Cut each sandwich on the diagonal. Dust with confectioners' sugar and serve with a side of jelly or sweet mustard. Makes 2

For a sweeter take, use egg bread and serve with dusted confectioners' sugar, fruit jellies, and fresh fruit. For a more savory version, use white or wheat bread, skip the confectioners' sugar and fruit, and serve with a side of mayo or sweet mustard and some sliced pickles.

Muffinwich

Nuffin's better than a muffin

When you hear "muffin sandwich," chances are good that English muffins come to mind. But traditional muffins like blueberry, lemon-poppy seed, and Morning Glory bring a lot more charm and playfulness to the breakfast table. Muffin sandwiches can be sweet or savory, so experiment with your favorite combos. Here are some tasty fillers to get you started: butter, whipped cream cheese, peanut butter, almond butter, Nutella, ricotta and mascarpone cheeses, and jams, jellies, and marmalades.

6 blueberry muffins (see opposite)
¾ cup whipped cream cheese
6 tablespoons orange marmalade
⅓ cup fresh blueberries

Slice each muffin in half. On bottom of each, spread 2 tablespoons cream cheese. Top each with 1 tablespoon marmalade and a few blueberries. Close sandwiches and serve. Makes 6

More Stuffins for Muffins

- Blueberry or raspberry muffins with whipped cream cheese, cooked bacon, and a drizzle of maple syrup
- Morning Glory or zucchini muffins with cooked eggs, a slice of ham, and a slice of cheddar
- Chocolate chip or peanut butter muffins with peanut butter, grilled bananas, and Nutella

- Cranberry-orange muffins with ricotta cheese, orange marmalade, and chopped walnuts
- Apple-spice muffins with almond butter, raisins, and Swiss cheese

Blueberry Muffins

½ cup (1 stick) butter
1¼ cups plus 1 teaspoon sugar, divided
½ teaspoon salt
2 large eggs
2 cups all-purpose flour
2 teaspoons baking powder
½ cup whole milk
1 teaspoon vanilla extract
1 teaspoon cinnamon
1 pint blueberries, rinsed and patted dry

❶ Place a rack in center of oven and preheat to 375°F. Coat a 6-cup muffin tin with cooking spray.

❷ Using a hand mixer, mix butter, 1¼ cups of the sugar, and salt until soft. Add eggs and mix until light and fluffy. In a separate bowl, combine flour and baking powder; in alternating addtions, stir flour mixture and milk into batter. Stir in vanilla and mix until just incorporated.

❸ In a small bowl, sprinkle cinnamon and the remaining 1 teaspoon of sugar over blueberries, toss until coated, and fold into batter. Spoon batter into muffin cups.

❹ Bake 25 to 30 minutes, or until tops are light gold and a cake tester inserted into the center of a muffin comes out clean. Transfer pan to a rack to cool 5 minutes; then remove each muffin to a wire rack to cool. Makes 6 muffins

M
N

Muffinwich

Muffuletta
"The Muff"

This bruiser of a sandwich is composed of a large, round loaf of crusty Italian bread filled with Italian meats and cheeses. It is distinguished from other Italian submarine-style sandwiches by the round (rather than oblong) loaf of bread and the addition of marinated olive salad—a chopped mixture of pimientos, celery, garlic, vinegar, and herbs.

If the **Po'boy** is New Orleans' signature Creole sandwich, the Muffuletta is its signature Italian sandwich—Sicilian to be exact. In the early 1900s, an influx of Sicilian immigrants arrived in New Orleans. One such newcomer, Lupo Salvatore, opened Central Grocery in 1906 and created the Muffuletta when he added olives to the bread of his Italian meat sandwiches. The name derives from the original bread used for the sandwiches, which was created by an Albanian baker. Today, few New Orleans bakeries sell the bread; other round, dense Italian or French loaves are used instead. Muffulettas are sold everywhere, from food trucks to pizzerias, though sticklers for authenticity still swear by Central Grocery.

Despite its dainty nickname, "muff," this sandwich is pure machismo. One is big enough to feed 2 or 3 people, but don't feel guilty about not sharing. And don't skip the beer to wash it all down.

---

1 (10-inch) round loaf Italian bread
¼ pound sliced Genoa salami
¼ pound sliced mortadella
¼ pound sliced hot or sweet capicola
¼ pound sliced sharp provolone cheese
Olive salad (opposite), with some of its oil
    drained and reserved

❶ Slice bread in half and scoop out some of the soft center to make room for the fillings. Brush insides with oil reserved from the olive salad.

❷ Starting with salami, layer meats and cheese on bottom half of bread. Top with a generous amount of olive salad. Place top half of bread on sandwich and press down firmly, without crushing the bread. Slice into 4 equal wedges.

❸ If feeling generous, share with a friend or two; if not, loosen your belt buckle and get started. Makes 1 monster sandwich

Olive Salad

Olive salad must be made at least 48 hours prior to eating, so plan accordingly. If you're short on time, many delis and supermarkets sell it alraedy prepared; some bottles are even labeled "for muffuletta sandwiches." You can use various combinations of Italian deli meats and cheeses in the sandwich—just make sure you have the olive salad, or it ain't a Muffuletta. Giardiniera is an Italian pickled salad available at specialty and regular markets.

1½ cups pitted green olives
½ cup pitted kalamata olives
1 cup store-bought giardiniera
2 tablespoons capers, drained
1 garlic clove, thinly sliced
¼ cup sliced, pickled cocktail onions
3 tablespoons red wine vinegar
1 tablespoon finely chopped fresh parsley
2 teaspoons dried oregano
¼ cup finely diced celery
¼ cup diced roasted red peppers
1 to 1½ cups olive oil

❶ In a large food processor, combine olives, giardiniera, capers, garlic, onions, vinegar, parsley, and oregano. Pulse several times until slightly chunky. Stir in celery and peppers. Transfer to a container with a tight-fitting lid.

❷ Pour olive oil over salad until completely covered; stir, close cover tightly, and refrigerate at least 48 hours and up to 1 week before using.
Makes 4 cups

M
N

Nutella Sandwich

A dreamy, decadent snack

Nutella is a sumptuous chocolate-hazelnut spread that was created in Italy but is enjoyed worldwide. The most common Nutella Sandwich consists simply of two slices of toasted bread that are slathered with the spread. Other fillings, such as grilled bananas, fruit jellies, and fresh berries, are popular pairings.

Chocolate and hazelnuts have been mingling happily since the 1800s. It wasn't until 1946, however, that the seeds for Nutella—that uniquely sweet, easily spreadable concoction—were sown. That's when Pietro Ferrero, who owned a bakery in Alba, Italy, began grinding hazelnuts into chocolate. First he created a solid block, but in 1949 he introduced a spread, which he labeled *supercrema* and first sold in 1951. In 1964 the spread was officially christened "Nutella," creating an instant sensation that continues to grow in popularity across the world. Though cheap imitations are available, none come close to the original: Nutella is the crème de la crème of creamy chocolate-hazelnut spreads.

1 loaf ciabatta or other crunchy bread, sliced on the thin side
1 jar Nutella
Kosher salt, to taste

❶ Place an indoor grill pan or a large skillet over medium heat. Grill bread 2 minutes per side, or until golden and crisp. Place toasted bread on a clean work surface.

❷ Spread 2 tablespoons Nutella on each piece of toast. Sprinkle with salt and close sandwiches. Eat while they're hot. Makes 4 to 6, depending on size of bread and thickness of slices

Everyone ❤s Nutella

- Peanut Butter and Nutella: Improve the classic PB&J by using Nutella instead of jelly.
- Banana and Nutella: Sauté sliced bananas in butter until golden and pair with Nutella.
- Fresh Fruit and Nutella: Add sliced fresh fruit, such as figs and ripe pears, or fresh berries.

Oyster Loaf

The classic Cajun-Creole supper

Originally, an Oyster Loaf consisted of a hollowed-out loaf of French bread coated with tartar sauce and stuffed till overflowing with crispy deep-fried oysters. Today this New Orleans specialty is typically served on a 6-inch roll split down the middle or on two hearty slices of bread. In some eateries, the name is used interchangeably with oyster **Po'boy**.

In his book *James Beard's American Cookery* (1972), the famed chef and author said that the Oyster Loaf "was what gentlemen who lingered too long in their favorite bar took home to the little woman as a peace offering." According to Beard, there were originally two types: one with fried oysters, the other with creamed oysters. One of the first printed recipes for this Creole dish dates back to the 1904 *Blue Grass Cook Book*, compiled by Minnie C. Fox. She advises filling a hollowed-out loaf of bread with 1 quart of fried oysters, ½ teacup of tomato catsup, and ½ dozen small pickles or 1 dozen olives. She adds that it makes "a nice supper dish after the theatre."

---

2 loaves toasted French bread
2 cups tartar sauce (page 186)
32 fried oysters (page 186)
4 pickled okra pods, sliced into thin rounds
Shredded lettuce
12 slices tomato

❶ Using a serrated knife, slice bread into 4 (6-inch) sections and in half lengthwise. Generously coat insides with tartar sauce.

❷ Arrange oysters on bottom; top with okra rounds. Sprinkle with lettuce; add tomato slices. Close sandwich. Makes 4

This recipe is reprinted with permission from Terry Thompson's cookbook *Cajun-Creole Cooking*, in which she posits that "no visit to New Orleans would ever be complete without at least one oyster loaf."

Homemade Tartar Sauce

1 to 1¼ cups mayonnaise
⅓ cup chopped dill pickles
¼ cup chopped pimiento-stuffed olives
½ small onion, minced
1 tablespoon fresh lemon juice
½ teaspoon salt
½ teaspoon freshly ground black pepper
½ teaspoon sugar

Combine all ingredients in a 2-quart bowl. Cover with plastic wrap; refrigerate until ready to serve (up to 2 days). Makes 2 cups

Crispy Fried Oysters

About ½ cup vegetable oil
32 shucked medium oysters, drained well
3 cups yellow cornmeal
1½ teaspoons salt
1½ teaspoons freshly ground black pepper
1 teaspoon cayenne pepper
2 cups all-purpose flour
2 eggs
2 cups milk

❶ Heat 3 inches of oil in a large saucepan to 365°F. Pat oysters dry on paper towel. In a shallow bowl, combine cornmeal, salt, pepper, and cayenne. Place flour in a second shallow bowl. In a third, beat together eggs and milk.

❷ Dredge dried oysters in flour; shake off excess. Dip each floured oyster in egg mixture. Dredge in seasoned cornmeal to coat well; shake off excess.

❸ Fry oysters in hot oil, 2 or 3 at a time, until crust is golden brown and crisp, 3 to 4 minutes. Drain on a wire rack. Makes 32 fried oysters, enough for 4 sandwiches

O
P

Panini

Scrumptious pressed sandwiches

In Italian, a *panino* is a "small bread roll" and refers to one sandwich, whereas *panini* refers to many sandwiches. In English, however, *panini* refers to one sandwich and *paninis* designates many. An American panini is a sandwich filled with any variety of meats, cheeses, and vegetables that is either pressed or cooked in a panini press, a waffle-iron-like grilling contraption.

In Italy, panini come in many varieties, though cured meats like prosciutto and salami are noted favorites. Panini are the classic café meal and can be found in many regions of Italy. American paninis have soared in popularity, particularly in the last decade, and have even become the subject of entire cookbooks and websites.

If you do not have a panini press, use a wide, heavy spatula to press firmly on the sandwich as it cooks; flip and repeat on the opposite side. Alternatively, place a heavy pan on the sandwich as it cooks; flip and repeat.

Panini

2 (½-inch-thick) slices eggplant
2 (½-inch-thick) slices zucchini
2 (½-inch-thick) slices red onion
½ red bell pepper, cut into 4 equal pieces
About 1 tablespoon olive oil, divided
Salt and freshly ground black pepper

BASIL MAYO
About 1 tablespoon mayonnaise
2 large fresh basil leaves, thinly sliced
Pinch crushed red pepper flakes

1 (6- to 8-inch) French baguette,
  split lengthwise
2 ounces crumbled goat cheese
  or fresh mozzarella

❶ Preheat grill to medium-high. Place sliced vegetables on a large plate or cookie sheet; brush with 2 teaspoons of the olive oil and season generously with salt and black pepper. Place on grill rack and close cover. Grill 5 to 7 minutes; flip and grill another 5 to 7 minutes, or until lightly charred and tender. Meanwhile, in a small bowl, mix mayo, basil, and crushed red pepper flakes; set aside.

❷ Brush inside of baguette with the remaining teaspoon olive oil. Place bread halves, cut side up, on a clean work surface. Spread each half with basil mayo. Divide vegetables evenly between halves and top with cheese. Close sandwich and place in panini press. Close the cover firmly and cook 3 to 5 minutes, or until bread is golden and cheese begins to melt. Cut on the diagonal. Serve hot. Makes 1

O
P

Savory and Sweet Panini Fillings

- Brie, apples, and honey
- Grilled chicken, fig jam, and fresh mozzarella
- PB&J
- Peanut butter, dark chocolate, and sea salt
- Roast beef, caramelized onions, and Gouda
- Serrano ham, sliced peaches or apricots, caramelized onions, and arugula
- Steak with caramelized onions, blue cheese, and horseradish sauce
- Strawberries, ricotta, and Nutella

Pastrami on Rye

An icon of Jewish deli cuisine

This New York deli specialty is a thick mound of hot pastrami, glistening with crisp fat, piled on top of two slices of rye bread and dressed with a spread of spicy mustard. If you think 6 ounces of pastrami sounds like a lot for one sandwich, think again. Many of New York's most famous delis pride themselves on their gargantuan pastrami sandwiches. This is a case where bigger really is better.

From 1880 to 1920, an influx of Jewish immigrants in New York introduced their culinary treasures to their new country. During the late 1800s, Eastern European Jews began flavoring and smoking corned beef (a brined meat made from brisket, the marbled, fatty portion of meat from the cow's breast). They applied a rub (made from a combination of spices that often became secret recipes among families) and smoked the meat for several hours. They called it "pastrami" and typically served it with spicy mustard on rye bread. The sandwich didn't reach the wider population until the early 1900s, when New York delis exploded onto the culinary scene. More than a century later, Pastrami on Rye is still considered an iconic New York Jewish deli food. In Montreal, a similar sandwich is known as the smoked meat.

2 teaspoons butter
2 slices rye bread
1 to 2 tablespoons spicy mustard
6 ounces sliced pastrami

❶ Butter both slices of bread and toast until golden. Spread mustard on both slices.

❷ Warm pastrami in a hot skillet until heated through. Pile on top of one slice of the bread and carefully close sandwich. Makes 1

To make a cold pastrami on rye, skip buttering and toasting the bread and place the meat cold on the sandwich.

Patty Melt

Quick and easy diner fare

A melt sandwich consists of bread, a filling, and a layer of cheese. A closed melt is grilled or fried in a pan until the cheese melts. An open-faced melt is placed under the broiler until the cheese melts. The two most popular are the Patty Melt (made with a hamburger, grilled onions, and cheese) and the Tuna Melt (see page 269).

The Patty Melt evolved sometime in the 1940s as an offshoot of the Cheeseburger (see page 126), which was originally served on toast. Traditionally, it is served on toasted rye bread and smothered with caramelized grilled onions and melted Swiss cheese. This mainstay of diner menus is so delicious that condiments such as mustard and ketchup are served on the side rather than on the sandwich.

---

2 tablespoons unsalted butter
1 small yellow onion, thinly sliced
1 (¼-pound) hamburger patty
1 slice Swiss cheese
2 slices buttered, toasted rye bread

❶ In a large skillet over medium-high heat, melt butter. Add onions and cook, stirring occasionally, until caramelized, about 15 minutes.

❷ In a large skillet or grill pan over medium-high heat, cook patty to desired doneness. Top with cheese and place on 1 slice of bread. Top with onions. Close sandwich. Eat it while it's hot. Makes 1

O
P

If you decide to make an open-faced sandwich, preheat the broiler while assembling the sandwich. Top the bread with the patty, onions, and cheese. Broil 2 to 3 minutes, or until the cheese melts. Don't forget the forks and knives.

Patty Melt Deluxe

- For a bacon and mushroom patty melt, add sautéed mushrooms and a slice of cooked bacon.
- For a healthy veggie melt, substitute a veggie burger for the beef and garnish with sauteed peppers, onions, and mushrooms.

- For that 1950s diner feel, pair your Patty Melt with crisp, golden French fries and a thick vanilla milkshake.
- For a taste of the Pacific Northwest, substitute a salmon patty for the beef and top with mayo, dill, pickle relish, and Swiss cheese.

Stephen Colbert claims to have invented a never-ending sandwich called the Mobius Melt: a grilled cheese sandwich, made with two other grilled cheese sandwiches as bread "and so on, in an endlessly recursive series of dual-state cheese-sandwich-bread sandwiches, extending into infinity."

Peanut Butter and Jelly
The homey American favorite

A Peanut Butter and Jelly sandwich consists of two slices of white bread joined harmoniously by a generous spread of smooth or chunky peanut butter and fruit jelly.

No one can deny that this sandwich, affectionately known as PB&J, is America's staple lunchtime sandwich. According to Andrew Smith, author of the 2002 book *The Illustrious History of the Goober Pea*, the first reference to the now iconic sandwich was published by Julia Davis Chandler in 1901. During the early twentieth century, peanut butter was considered a delicacy; it wasn't until the introduction of mass-produced peanut butter in the 1920s that it became the humble American favorite we know today. During the Great Depression, American moms sent their children to school with inexpensive yet filling PB&Js, though the sandwich got its big break during World War II: Apparently, GIs preferred to combine their rationed jelly with rationed peanut butter, making for a less sticky, more delicious concoction. After the war, the GIs were hooked, and they successfully helped brand the PB&J as a beloved signature American sandwich. Although favored by children and adults alike, they are ultimately considered the quintessential kid's lunch.

About 3 tablespoons peanut butter, or to taste
2 slices white bread
Jelly, to taste (purists insist on grape)

Spread peanut butter on both slices of bread. Top 1 slice with a liberal amount of jelly. Close sandwich and eat. Makes 1

Mix 'n' Match!

Bread	Butter	Jelly	And More
French country white	Almond butter	Apricot preserves	Marshmallow Fluff
Sourdough	Cashew butter	Raspberry jam	Chocolate shavings
Rye	Nutella	Fig jam	Caramel
Cut into fun shapes	Sunflower butter	Rose's lime jelly	Fresh sliced fruit
with cookie cutters	Apple butter	Lemon curd	Raisins or dried
Bagel			apricots

Peanut Butter and Jelly

O
P

O
P

Peanut Butter Sandwich

More than just a PB&J without the jelly

A Peanut Butter Sandwich typically consists of two slices of white bread bound together by a liberal spread of smooth or chunky peanut butter. Popular variations include peanut butter and bacon, peanut butter and pickles, peanut butter and mayo, and peanut butter and lettuce.

According to food historian Andrew Smith, European explorers discovered peanuts in the New World and introduced them to Africa, where they were used as food in the slave trade. Eventually they were introduced to the British North American colonies. In America, peanut butter was originally touted as a health food by vegetarian John Harvey Kellogg. His "nut butter" became associated with both the health-conscious and the affluent, and by 1900 peanut butter sandwiches made with fillings such as raisins, apricots, bacon, and pimiento were being served regularly at fashionable restaurants. With the introduction of mass-produced peanut butter in the 1920s, the once high-brow food became more democratic. As an inexpensive source of protein during the Great Depression and World War II, peanut butter quickly became one of America's favorite foods.

About 3 tablespoons peanut butter, or to taste
2 slices white bread
Any desired fillings

Spread a liberal amount of peanut butter on bread. Top with your choice of ingredients. Close sandwich and eat. Makes 1

Mix 'n' Match!

Choose from among the following fillings, or create your own:

Bread	*Filling*	
Sourdough	Pickle chips	Sliced celery or carrots
Rye	Cooked bacon strips	Sliced apples
Crusty Italian	Sliced deli meats (bologna	Banana and honey
Brioche	or ham)	Dates, raisins, or apricots
	Iceberg lettuce and mayo	Potato chips
		Chocolate chips

O
P

Pepper and Egg Sandwich

Economy + deliciousness

This sandwich consists of soft scrambled eggs that are seasoned with sautéed garlic, onions, and green bell peppers, all tucked inside a toasted crusty roll. Though it's perfect as is, regional preferences for adornments include melted mozzarella or sharp provolone, pickled pepperoncini, giardiniera (a spicy blend of pickled vegetables), and marinara sauce.

A classic Italian "peasant dish," the Pepper and Egg Sandwich is an example of economy and deliciousness colliding. Historically, the sandwich was a nourishing yet inexpensive meal for large families and has always been particularly popular during the Lenten season, when many Catholics abstain from eating meat on Fridays. Although it goes by different regional names, most people drop the "sandwich" part, calling it simply "eggs and peppers" or, more accurately, "peppiz 'n' eggz."

You can substitute sweet banana peppers (long, tapered, yellow peppers) for the green bell peppers, or add diced cooked pancetta or bacon. Peppers and eggs should be made just before eating so that you can fully appreciate the contrasting textures of the hot, fluffy scrambled eggs against the crisp and crusty bread.

---

1 (12-inch) loaf crusty bread or 2 (6-inch) torpedo rolls, sliced lengthwise but still attached

1 tablespoon olive oil, divided

6 eggs

⅛ teaspoon salt

⅛ teaspoon black pepper

1 teaspoon minced garlic

1 medium yellow onion, thinly sliced

1 medium green bell pepper, thinly sliced

4 slices mozzarella or sharp provolone (optional)

❶ Preheat broiler. Drizzle bread with 1 teaspoon olive oil; broil 2 to 3 minutes or until golden.

❷ In a bowl, whisk eggs, salt, and pepper. In a medium skillet over medium heat, add remaining 2 teaspoons olive oil. Add garlic and onions and sauté 1 to 2 minutes. Add peppers and sauté 3 to 5 minutes, or until soft. Add eggs. Using a spatula, stir occasionally, 2 to 3 minutes, or until eggs are no longer runny. Place sliced cheese in bread, if using. Top with eggs. Serve hot. Makes 1 (12-inch) sandwich or 2 (6-inch) sandwiches

O
P

Pepper and Egg Sandwich

O
P

Philly Cheesesteak

Philly Cheesesteak
The king of sandwiches

Referred to simply as cheesesteak by locals, this sandwich consists of thin slices of steak topped with melted cheese (white American, provolone, or Cheez Whiz) and sometimes includes sliced onions and sweet or hot peppers.

Pat Olivieri, owner of a hot dog stand in South Philadelphia, was tired of eating hot dogs for lunch every day. So one day in 1930 he grilled some steak and onions and packed it inside an Italian roll. A cabbie friend drove by, spotted the sandwich, and asked for one to go. Legend has it that the cabbie took one bite and told Olivieri to forget about the dogs and go with the steak sandwiches. He did. In the late 1940s he added cheese to the sandwich, creating the cheesesteak. Today Pat's King of Steaks is still located in the heart of South Philly and has become a city icon. Unlike most sandwiches, there *is* a correct way to order a cheesesteak. Do it wrong, and you'll get yelled at by the person taking your order.

1. Know what you want before getting in line.
2. Don't smile or dilly-dally when it's time to order.
3. Order like a local, and keep it to three words. The first word is *one*, which means you're ordering one sandwich. The second indicates the type of cheese you want. And the third is either *wit* or *witout*, which indicates your preference for fried onions. So "one, Whiz, wit" is a cheesesteak with Cheez Whiz and fried onions.

If you get the wrong sandwich, don't say anything. Just eat it. Or get back in line and try again. Also, don't be surprised if you do everything correctly and still get yelled at. It's part of the Philly cheesesteak experience. For the best-tasting cheesesteaks, buy top-quality bread, preferably at an Italian specialty market, and top-quality fresh, not frozen, meat.

2 tablespoons olive oil

1 large yellow onion, thinly sliced

1 green bell pepper, sliced into thin strips

2 cups white button mushrooms, thinly sliced

1¼ pounds rib eye (or top sirloin or round), sliced very thinly

Salt and freshly ground black pepper

4 hoagie rolls, split lengthwise

8 ounces (or 8 slices) cheese, such as Cheez Whiz, sliced provolone, or sliced American

Garnishes of your choice, such as ketchup, hot peppers, or sliced pickles

❶ Add oil to a large skillet over medium heat. Sauté onions, peppers, and mushrooms 5 minutes, or until lightly browned. Add steak and sauté 5 minutes, or until tender and no longer pink. Season generously with salt and pepper.

❷ Working with 1 roll at a time, add 2 ounces of the cheese. Scoop in steak mixture and top with your choice of garnishes, plus extra cheese if you'd like. Eat it while it's hot. Makes 4

There's a Cheesesteak for Everyone

- Chicken Cheesesteak: Use diced chicken breast instead of steak for a beef-free alternative.
- Buffalo Chicken Cheesesteak: Season chicken with hot sauce before filling sandwich; top it off with blue cheese dressing.
- Pizza Steak: Top Cheesesteak with pizza sauce, shredded mozzarella, and other favorite pizza toppings; place sandwich under the broiler to melt cheese.

- Cheesesteak Hoagie: Combine Philly's two favorites by lining the roll with shredded lettuce, tomato slices, raw onion, and mayonnaise before piling on the meat and cheese.
- Chipotle Cheesesteak: Add a spoonful of chopped chipotle peppers in adobo sauce to the sandwich.

If one giant cheesesteak isn't enough, take the South Philly Challenge: a wide slice of Lorenzo's pizza wrapped around an entire cheesesteak and consumed in under an hour—usually after a long night out on the town.

Po'boy

New Orleans' pride and joy

A classic Po'boy is a **Submarine Sandwich** distinguished by its bread: fresh New Orleans French bread that is golden and crunchy on the outside and light and airy on the inside. This perfect vessel holds any number of fillings, from fried seafood, such as shrimp, oysters, and catfish, to meats like roast beef, Italian sausage, and ham.

How did this signature sandwich get its name? There are too many competing legends to cite. Most food historians credit brothers Benny and Clovis Martin, who opened the Martin Brothers Grocery in New Orleans in the 1920s. When streetcar workers went on strike in 1929, the Martins created the Po'boy as a hearty, inexpensive meal for these so-called poor boys. Eventually the phrase was shortened to *po'boys*, reflecting the city's dialect. The sandwich's popularity quickly spread, and by the 1930s it could be found at food trucks and lunch counters throughout the city. Today Po'boys are available at eateries across the United States, though it's hard to beat the ones from N'awlins.

O
P

Po'boys can come "dressed" with mayo, lettuce, tomato, and pickles; "hot," made with a spicy Creole mustard; or "regular," adorned simply with yellow mustard.

FRIED SHRIMP

1½ to 2 pounds shrimp (about 28 total,
   7 for each sandwich)

1 egg

⅓ cup milk

2 teaspoons hot sauce, plus more for serving

½ cup all-purpose flour

2 tablespoons Old Bay seasoning

1 cup cornmeal

3 to 4 cups canola oil

4 sub rolls, split lengthwise

8 leaves Bibb lettuce

8 thin slices tomato

½ cup melted butter

❶ Peel and devein shrimp; rinse and pat dry. In a small bowl, whisk together egg, milk, and hot sauce. In a separate bowl, mix flour and Old Bay seasoning. Place cornmeal in a third bowl. Place 1 shrimp at a time in egg mixture, then flour, then cornmeal until completely coated. Place on a large plate until ready to fry.

❷ Pour oil at least 2 inches deep in a heavy-bottomed pan and heat to 350°F. Fry shrimp in batches 1 to 2 minutes, or until golden and crisp. Place on a paper-towel-lined plate until ready to eat.

❸ Place 1 roll on a clean work surface. Add 2 lettuce leaves, 2 tomato slices, and 7 shrimp. Assemble remaining sandwiches. Drizzle with hot melted butter and a few dashes of hot sauce. Eat immediately. Makes 4

O
P

Shrimp Po'boys, like other fried seafood Po'boys, come either dressed with lettuce, tomato, and pickles or topped with melted butter and hot sauce.

Po'boy

O
P

Pork Tenderloin Sandwich

This little piggy tastes great

Also called a breaded pork sandwich or "the Iowa skinny," this Midwestern favorite is identifiable by a monstrous, breaded, fried slab of pork tenderloin that overwhelms a hamburger bun or kaiser roll and is dressed simply with mayo, onions, and pickles.

Not unlike the **Chicken-Fried Steak Sandwich**, the Pork Tenderloin Sandwich is an offshoot of German wiener schnitzel (thin, bread-crumb-coated pieces of veal that are then fried), which was introduced to North America in the mid-nineteenth century by German immigrants. It was created by Nick Freinstein, a sandwich peddler in Huntington, Indiana, who opened his own restaurant, Nick's Kitchen, in 1908. According to authors Jane and Michael Stern, Nick's brother Jake, who had lost his fingers from severe frostbite, used his stumps to tenderize the pork loin. Eventually, mechanized tenderizing tools became standard, ensuring consistently tender, juicy pieces of meat. More than a century later, Nick's is still serving its customers Pork Tenderloin Sandwiches made with the original recipe.

BREADED PORK

1 (4- to 6-ounce) pork tenderloin cutlet

1 egg

2 tablespoons milk

⅛ teaspoon salt

⅛ teaspoon black pepper

2 tablespoons all-purpose flour

2 tablespoons cornmeal

2 tablespoons canola oil

1 tablespoon mayonnaise

1 hamburger bun or kaiser roll

5 or 6 pickle chips

2 or 3 slices white onion

❶ Trim meat of fat. Using the flat side of a meat mallet, pound to ⅛ inch thick. In a small bowl, whisk together egg, milk, salt, and pepper. Place flour in one shallow plate and cornmeal in another.

❷ Warm oil in a large skillet over medium heat. Dip meat into egg mixture. Dredge in flour. Dip in egg again, then dredge in cornmeal until completely coated. Place in hot oil. Fry 3 to 4 minutes, flip, and fry 2 to 3 minutes more, or until golden brown. Spread mayo inside bun and place meat on bottom half. Top with pickles and onion and close sandwich. Eat it while it's hot. Makes 1

Potato Chip Sandwich

A crunchy salty guilty pleasure

Known as a crisp sandwich in the United Kingdom, a Potato Chip Sandwich is any sandwich that includes an overlapping layer of potato chips. Many people like to match a flavored chip with a particular sandwich, such as barbecue chips on ham and cheddar, salt and vinegar chips on tuna fish, and plain chips on peanut butter.

Potato chips were invented in 1853 in Saratoga, New York, but it was the 1920 invention of the mechanical potato peeler that launched the chip industry. When moisture-resistant packaging was created soon after, potato chips could be shipped anywhere. It's impossible to identify the first person to place potato chips on a sandwich, but it's safe to say that virtually everyone has done it at one time or another. A recipe for one proudly appears in the 1986 cookbook *White Trash Cooking*. It may not be epicurean, but it sure tastes good.

Layer the chips and gently press the sandwich with the palm of your hand before biting into it. Otherwise, you could risk a puncture wound in the roof of your mouth, which will hurt like the dickens when the salt hits it.

---

2 tablespoons creamy peanut butter
2 slices white bread
4 to 6 dill pickle chips
A layer of your favorite plain potato chips

Spread peanut butter on both bread slices. Place pickle chips on one slice. Top with overlapping potato chips. Close sandwich and enjoy! Makes 1

Crunchy Delicious Variations

- Plain Jane: Spread mayo on white bread and top with potato chips.
- Banana Crunch: Spread peanut butter on white bread. Add sliced bananas, and top with potato chips.
- Cheese 'n' Chips: Make a grilled cheese sandwich with American cheese and potato chips on buttered white bread. This salty sandwich may be the best midnight snack of all time.

Potato Chip Sandwich

Pound Cake Sandwich

Pound Cake Sandwich

The ultimate dessert sandwich

A pound cake is a buttery white cake with a golden crust. Its name was derived from the measurement of ingredients traditionally used: one pound each of flour, butter, sugar, and eggs, according to British and American cookbooks dating back to the 1750s. As for the Pound Cake Sandwich, it was most likely invented by ingenious moms and grandmas looking for ways to use up leftover slices of cake. It is currently back in vogue thanks to celebrity chefs such as Gale Gand and Martha Stewart, who have offered their own sweet versions. This delightful snack is made by buttering and grilling two thick slabs of cake and sandwiching sweet ingredients, including whipped cream, fruity cream cheese, and melted chocolate.

MACERATED STRAWBERRIES

2 to 2½ cups fresh ripe strawberries, thinly sliced

¼ cup sugar, or to taste

3 tablespoons orange juice

Zest of 1 small orange

¼ teaspoon pure vanilla extract

About 2 tablespoons butter, divided

1 pound cake, sliced thin

1 (8-ounce) container whole-milk ricotta
   or mascarpone

❶ A few hours beforehand, prepare strawberries: In a glass bowl, combine all ingredients for macerated strawberries. Toss well. Let rest at room temperature at least 2 hours.

❷ Butter both sides of cake slices. Place on a hot buttered griddle; cook 2 minutes per side, or until golden. Remove from heat. For each sandwich, spread 2 tablespoons ricotta on 1 slice of grilled cake, top with a spoonful of berries, and close sandwich. Serve warm. Makes 4 to 6, depending on the thickness of the bread

Frozen strawberries can be substituted for fresh;
just reduce the amount of orange juice since frozen
berries will release more liquid.

Primanti

Fit a meal into a sandwich

From steel to the Steelers, Pittsburgh's contributions to the world have been significant, but one has changed sandwich culture forever. Founded in 1933, Primanti Bros. restaurant makes sandwiches that are Herculean: Two slices of bread struggle to contain a mountain of meat, French fries, vinegar-based coleslaw, and tomatoes.

The first Primanti restaurant wasn't a restaurant at all; it was a sparse wooden lunch stand run by Joe Primanti and his nephew John DePriter during the Great Depression, when the city's produce was delivered in the middle of the night. "One winter, a fella drove in with a load of potatoes," says DePriter. "He brought a few of 'em over to the restaurant to see if they were frozen. I fried the potatoes on our grill and they looked pretty good. A few customers asked for them, so I put the potatoes on their sandwiches." The gargantuan Primanti sandwich allowed them to enjoy a much-deserved meal with one hand while steering their trucks with the other.

---

4 ounces pastrami, turkey, roast beef
   or corned beef, or 1 (4-ounce) cooked
   ground-beef patty

1 slice provolone cheese
2 slices Italian bread
Handful of French fries
½ cup vinegar-based coleslaw
2 slices tomato

❶ Grill meat to warm through. When nearly done, top with cheese and continue to warm until cheese is melted.

❷ Place meat and cheese on top of 1 bread slice. Add fries, then coleslaw, then tomato slices, and top with second bread slice.
Makes 1

According to Amy Smith of Primanti Bros., "We've become a kind of cult. You just *have* to have a Primanti sandwich when you're in Pittsburgh."

Primanti

O
P

Prosciutto and Fig Sandwich

O
P

Prosciutto and Fig Sandwich

Gourmet sandwich perfection

A prosciutto sandwich consists of paper-thin slices of prosciutto, an Italian cured ham, served on crusty bread, such as ciabatta. It is often paired with figs, cheese, and fresh herbs and usually dressed with extra-virgin olive oil and aged balsamic vinegar.

Italians' passion for *prosciutto di Parma* (prosciutto made in Parma) has deep roots: The writings of Cato, which date to approximately 100 BCE, describe the process of curing pork legs in barrels of salt before drying and smoking the meat. Today Parma, a city in Emilia-Romagna, is considered the preeminent maker of prosciutto, which is prized for its delicate flavor and melt-in-your-mouth tenderness.

---

1 teaspoon extra-virgin olive oil
2 thin slices ciabatta bread
4 paper-thin slices prosciutto
1½ tablespoons goat cheese
1 ripe fresh fig, thinly sliced, or 1 tablespoon
    fig marmalade
Several fresh arugula leaves
Freshly ground black pepper, to taste

Drizzle oil on both bread slices. Place prosciutto on 1 slice. Top with goat cheese, fig slices, and arugula leaves. Season with pepper. Close sandwich and serve. Makes 1

Other Prosciutto Sandwiches

- Pair prosciutto with olive tapenade and smoked Gouda cheese on focaccia.
- Layer slices of prosciutto and fresh basil leaves on ciabatta bread and drizzle with extra-virgin olive oil.

- Make a panini by spreading basil pesto on Italian bread and filling it with prosciutto and fresh mozzarella cheese.
- Layer slices of prosciutto with slices of ripe peach or nectarine and basil or arugula.

O
P

Pulled Pork Sandwich

Hearty BBQ to feed a crowd

Pulled pork is a type of barbecue: pork butt (the pig's shoulder) cooked slowly over low heat until tender enough to be pulled into small pieces. This sandwich is traditionally composed of a generous amount of pulled pork piled high on an untoasted white roll. It's usually topped with lots of barbecue sauce and may come topped with a scoop of creamy coleslaw or a few pickle slices.

The Pulled Pork Sandwich is most closely associated with the southern United States, which boasts an entire barbecue lexicon. There are many regional recipes for pulled pork that vary according to cooking methods (smokers, ovens, crock pots) and sauce styles (vinegar-based, tomato-based, mustard-based). Regardless of regional differences, all great pulled pork sandwiches have a few things in common: succulent meat, ample barbeque sauce, and plain bread. Eating one is a wonderfully sloppy affair. Have a large stack of napkins nearby and—whatever you do—avoid wearing white!

COLESLAW
12 cups shredded green cabbage
½ cup unseasoned rice vinegar
½ cup light brown sugar
2 teaspoons olive oil
A generous sprinkling of salt and freshly ground
    black pepper to taste

8 to 10 cups pulled pork, shredded (page 219)
8 to 10 hamburger buns or kaiser rolls
Extra barbecue sauce, for serving (optional)
Pickle slices

❶ To make coleslaw, place cabbage in a large bowl. In a small pot over medium-high heat, bring vinegar and brown sugar to a boil. Reduce to a simmer and add oil, salt, and pepper. Simmer 3 to 5 minutes. Pour over cabbage. Refrigerate until ready to use (it can be made up to a week in advance).

❷ Place about 1 cup meat on each bun. Drizzle with extra barbecue sauce, if desired. Top with a scoop of coleslaw and some pickle slices. Close sandwiches and eat immediately. Makes 8 to 10

Serve with pickles, coleslaw, baked beans, or French fries.

Pulled Pork Sandwich

Pulled Pork

No special kitchen equipment required, just your oven. For a super-fast version, purchase cooked shredded pork, which is available at most Mexican specialty markets as well as some major supermarkets.

MEAT RUB

4 tablespoons light brown sugar
1 teaspoon onion powder
4 teaspoons salt
2 teaspoons black pepper
2 teaspoons dry mustard
2 tablespoons paprika
2 tablespoons chipotle chili powder

1 (5- to 7-pound) boneless pork shoulder
 or Boston butt roast

TANGY VINEGAR BARBECUE SAUCE

1½ cups apple cider vinegar
1 cup ketchup
⅔ cup light brown sugar
2 tablespoons Tabasco
¼ cup stone-ground mustard

❶ In a small bowl, combine rub ingredients and stir until well blended. Using your fingertips, rub mixture over meat. Refrigerate at least 2 hours and preferably overnight. Remove from refrigerator 20 minutes before cooking.

❷ Preheat oven to 250°F. Place meat, fat side up, on the rack of a shallow roasting pan. Cook uncovered 2 hours. Raise oven temperature to 350°F. Cover meat with tinfoil and cook another 5 to 6 hours, or until internal temperature reaches 170°F and meat is very tender. Remove meat from oven and place on a large cutting board or platter. Tent with a piece of tinfoil and let rest 20 to 30 minutes.

❸ In a small pot over medium-high heat, add barbecue sauce ingredients. Bring to a boil; lower heat and simmer 5 to 7 minutes, stirring occasionally. Pour sauce in a wide, shallow dish that is large enough to hold the meat. Uncover meat and shred into small pieces using a large fork. Transfer shredded meat to the dish with the barbecue sauce and toss to coat completely. Makes enough for 8 to 10 sandwiches

O
P

Reuben

The quintessential Jewish deli sandwich

This beauty consists of hot slices of corned beef that are topped with sauerkraut, Swiss cheese, and Russian or Thousand Island dressing, all nestled between two butter-toasted slices of rye bread. Made from beef brisket, corned beef has been cured in "corns" of salt. In the days before refrigeration, salting was a way to prevent meat from spoiling.

When a sandwich is as good as a Reuben, more than one person wants to take credit for its creation. In this case there are three competing versions. The first credits Arthur Reuben (1883–1970), founder of Reuben's Restaurant and Delicatessen in New York. The story goes that one evening in 1914 one of his customers, an actress named Anna Selos, asked for something hearty to eat. Reuben whipped up a hefty sandwich made with Virginia ham, turkey, Swiss cheese, coleslaw, and his special Russian dressing, christening his concoction the "Reuben Special." The second theory holds that Reuben Kulakofsky, a wholesale grocer from Nebraska, created the sandwich one night during a card game. Charles Schimmel, one of the players, was so smitten that he dubbed it "the Reuben" and put it on the menu at his hotel's restaurant, where it quickly gained fame. The third version claims the inventor was Fern Snider, grand-prize winner of a 1956 national sandwich idea contest.

For the best-tasting Reuben, buy corned beef from a quality deli.
The Rachel is a variation of the Reuben that substitutes pastrami and
creamy coleslaw for the corned beef and sauerkraut.

2 tablespoons butter, divided

2 thick slices rye bread

4 to 5 slices hot corned beef

2 tablespoons sauerkraut, drained and gently warmed

2 slices Swiss cheese

2 tablespoons Russian or Thousand Island dressing

❶ Butter bread slices on one side with half the butter. Place bread slices buttered side down. Top each with half the corned beef, then add sauerkraut and cheese.

❷ Spread dressing on top of cheese and close sandwich. In a skillet over medium heat, melt 1 tablespoon butter. Place sandwich in skillet and cook until browned and crisp, about 2 to 3 minutes. Carefully flip and toast the other side 1 to 2 minutes. Cut in half and serve immediately. Makes 1

Q
R

At Mader's German restaurant in Milwaukee, Wisconsin, you can get a reuben roll, also known as a reuben egg roll: corned beef, cabbage, and Swiss cheese tucked inside an egg roll wrapper and fried until golden and crisp.

Roast Beef

Don't skimp on the beef

This generous mound of thinly sliced roast beef is piled on sliced bread (usually white, rye, or pumpernickel) and dressed most popularly with a spread of creamy mayo and sharp horseradish.

Like the humble **Ham Sandwich**, the Roast Beef Sandwich can be found everywhere from baseball stadiums to tony bistros. When in 1964 Forrest and Leroy Raffel opened their first Arby's, a fast-food chain restaurant, they wanted to offer customers a delicious, satisfying all-American sandwich that wasn't a **Hamburger**. They succeeded by specializing in roast beef sandwiches. Today there are approximately 4,000 Arby's in the United States and Canada. Though the roast beef sandwich comes in many forms, most enthusiasts wouldn't dream of eating one without a liberal dousing of nose-tingling horseradish sauce—a creamy mixture of mayonnaise or sour cream and grated horseradish—which Arby's calls Horsey Sauce.

---

1 to 2 tablespoons store-bought horseradish sauce (depending on how much nose-tingling you can tolerate)

1 kaiser roll

3 ounces thinly sliced lean roast beef

2 slices Swiss cheese

2 slices tomato

3 slices red onion

❶ Spread horseradish sauce inside roll. Carefully pile roast beef on bottom of roll.

❷ Top with cheese, tomato, and onion. Close sandwich and serve. Makes 1

Roast Beef

QR

Roast Beef Deluxe

- Beef on Weck: To serve this Buffalo, New York, favorite, layer thinly sliced roast beef and horseradish on a kummelweck roll—a kaiser roll with kosher salt and caraway seeds—dipped in au jus.
- The Brazilian Bauru: Use French bread (with the soft interior removed) as a crunchy vessel for tomatoes, pickles, melted mozzarella cheese, and, of course, roast beef.
- California Roast Beef: For a California twist, serve roast beef on toasted multigrain bread with horseradish mayo, sliced raw red onion, fresh tomato slices, and watercress.

Brazilians take their roast beef sandwich so seriously that the recipe has been codified into local law in Bauru, the city that gave the sandwich its name.

Q
R

Salmon Sandwich

A modern take on the fish sandwich

A Salmon Sandwich consists of grilled, panfried, or broiled salmon fillets that are served on toasted bread and dressed with any number of garnishes, such as avocado slices, bacon strips, and pickle relish.

Touted for its health-promoting omega-3 fatty acids, salmon is considered a healthier alternative to traditional **Fish Sandwiches**. Consumption of fresh and frozen salmon rose considerably in the 1990s, and it continues to gain popularity worldwide. Myriad varieties of salmon sandwiches are available at restaurants and bistros, though the best-loved version remains the salmon BLT—not exactly healthy, but oh so good.

TARRAGON MAYO
¼ cup regular or light mayonnaise
1 teaspoon Dijon mustard
¼ teaspoon lemon juice
2 teaspoons finely chopped fresh tarragon
2 teaspoons finely chopped fresh chives

PANFRIED SALMON
2 teaspoons olive oil
2 (4- to 6-ounce) salmon fillets

4 slices sourdough or multigrain bread
¼ cup fresh watercress or arugula leaves
½ small ripe avocado, sliced

❶ For the tarragon mayo, combine all ingredients in a small bowl. Mix well and set aside.

❷ Warm oil in a large skillet over medium-high heat. Add salmon fillets and cook until just opaque in the center, about 3 to 4 minutes per side.

❸ Toast bread until golden; place 2 slices on a clean work surface. Spread tarragon mayo on each. Top with watercress, cooked salmon, and avocado. Close sandwiches and serve immediately. Makes 2

For a salmon BLT, add panfried salmon
to a traditional BLT.

Sandwich Loaf
Retro party food

This large multitiered party sandwich masquerades as a cake and makes more than enough to feed a crowd. It consists of an entire loaf of bread that is horizontally sliced and filled with creamy spreads such as tuna salad, egg salad, deviled ham, and pimiento cheese. The finished sandwich is—no kidding—frosted like a cake with cream cheese that is typically tinted a festive shade of green, blue, or red. Like a party cake, the loaf is decorated with colorful garnishes, including radish roses, fresh herbs, and olives. It became a popular party dish in the 1950s but generally fell out of favor after the 1970s. Is it a garish monster of a sandwich or a charmingly kitschy party snack? You decide.

---

1 (1-pound) loaf white bread, preferably day-old
½ cup (1 stick) softened butter,
    or more as needed
6 cups total creamy salads and/or spreads
    (use 2 cups of each)

FROSTING
2 (8-ounce) packages cream cheese
3 to 4 tablespoons milk, or as much as needed
A couple drops of green, blue, or red food
    coloring, optional

Your choice of garnishes, optional

❶ Using a serrated knife, trim crust from bread. Slice loaf lengthwise into 4 equal slices. Generously butter 1 side of each slice. Place the bottom bread slice on a serving platter, buttered side up. Spread a filling evenly on the slice.

❷ Top with the second bread slice, buttered side up, and spread an even layer of the next filling. Top with the third slice, buttered side up. Spread the last filling evenly on the slice and top with remaining bread slice.

❸ Stir together cream cheese and milk until mixture is thick yet spreadable. Stir in food coloring (if using). Frost sides and top of loaf and decorate with garnishes (if using). Chill until frosting is set, about 30 minutes. Slice, serve, and party! Makes 14 to 16 slices

S
T

Mix 'n' Match!

Salads	Spreads	Garnishes
Chicken salad	Nut spread	Sliced radishes
Tuna salad	Olive spread	Carrots
Egg salad	Pimento cheese	Cucumbers
Shrimp salad	Deviled ham	Celery
		Grapes
		Pickles
		Pimento olives
		Pickle relish
		Watercress
		Fresh herbs

Sardine Sandwich

Seriously robust flavor

A traditional Sardine Sandwich consists of chopped canned sardines that are mixed with spicy mustard and lemon and served with finely chopped onion on rye or whole wheat bread. Sardines are small fish of the herring family that are usually canned in oil or water. These sandwiches are most commonly eaten in the Midwest, where they were introduced by Scandinavian immigrants. Jewish delis and restaurants, mainly in New York, typically serve the sandwich on rye and call it "sardines on rye."

If you purchase canned sardines whole, you will have to remove the heads and firmly twist out the backbones before eating. Be aware that briny sardines and raw onions are a robust combination; even its most ardent admirers will tell you that the smell is as powerful as the flavor. If you're indulging in this sandwich for lunch, you may want to keep a tin of breath mints nearby.

---

2 ounces oil-packed boneless, skinless sardines, drained and chopped

1 teaspoon spicy mustard

¼ teaspoon lemon juice

Salt and freshly ground black pepper, to taste

2 thin slices rye bread

2 teaspoons mayonnaise, optional

1 tablespoon finely chopped red or white onion

2 slices hard-boiled egg, optional

❶ In a small bowl, mix chopped sardines, spicy mustard, lemon juice, salt, and pepper until combined. Spread on 1 slice of bread (with or without mayo).

❷ Top with chopped onions and, if using, egg slices. Close sandwich. Makes 1

S
T

Sardine Sandwich

Sausage and Pepper Sandwich

Sausage and Pepper Sandwich

Smothered links in a crusty roll

This modest Italian street food is a Neapolitan specialty that was introduced to America by Italian immigrants at the turn of the twentieth century. In many Italian American households, the sandwich is as familiar as **Peanut Butter and Jelly**, but it's a whole lot more filling. Some of the most memorable of these stuffed sandwiches are found at food trucks, ballpark concessions, and Italian street festivals, where you can usually just say, "Yeah, give me a soss-age 'n' peppiz, will ya?"

---

2 tablespoons olive oil

4 Italian sausage links (about 1¼ pounds total), preferably hot Italian sausage with fennel seeds

1 small green bell pepper, cut into thin strips

1 small red bell pepper, cut into thin strips

1 medium yellow onion, thinly sliced

Salt, to taste

¼ teaspoon crushed red pepper flakes

3 to 4 tablespoons red wine or water

4 sub rolls or crusty ciabatta rolls, split lengthwise

❶ Place oil in a large skillet over medium heat. Add sausage links and cook, turning until browned all over, about 5 minutes. Add bell peppers, onion, salt, and crushed red pepper flakes. Reduce heat to medium-low and sauté, turning occasionally, about 5 minutes. Add wine or water and cook until most of the liquid has evaporated, about 2 to 3 minutes. The meat should be thoroughly cooked and the vegetables tender.

❷ Brush rolls with olive oil and broil 1 to 2 minutes, or until golden and crisp.

❸ Open 1 roll. Place 1 sausage link firmly inside. Smother with a quarter of the peppers and onions. Repeat with remaining sandwiches. Eat immediately. Makes 4

Melted or Grilled, It's Tasty and Delicious

- Sausage and Pepper Melt: After assembling the sandwich, place 2 slices of mozzarella or sharp provolone on top of the onion-pepper mixture and top with 2 to 3 tablespoons of your favorite marinara sauce. Place under a broiler for 2 minutes until the cheese melts and the bread turns golden.

- Grilled Sausage and Pepper Sandwich: Preheat grill to medium. Grill sausages for 4 to 5 minutes per side or until browned and cooked through.

Christopher Columbus gave peppers their name
when he encountered them in North America,
mistaking them for a variety of Indian peppercorns.

S
T

Sliders

Scrumptious little snacks

These miniature sandwiches are served on small, round buns. Fillings range from beef to chicken to seafood, though just about any sandwich can be transformed into a slider.

Where did this little guy get its funky name? It's likely a nod to the original "slyder," the square **Hamburger** created in 1921 at White Castle, the Wichita, Kansas, restaurant chain. It may also refer to the ease with which the sandwich slides down into your belly. Whatever the reason, we can't seem to get enough of these petite treats. In the United States, they're available everywhere from fast-food chains to trendy bars and bistros.

---

9 ounces grass fed beef (or ground chuck, 85% lean)

Several shakes of salt and freshly ground black pepper

3 mini rolls or dinner rolls, split

2 to 3 tablespoons blue cheese dressing

½ cup fresh arugula

❶ Preheat grill to medium. Place meat in a bowl. Sprinkle with salt and black pepper. Gently form 3 equal patties, trying not to over-work meat.

❷ Place patties on grill. Cook 3 to 4 minutes; flip once, and cook another 3 to 4 minutes, or to desired level of doneness (140°F for medium-rare and 150°F for medium; the USDA recommends cooking beef to 160°F for maximum safety). Place 1 burger on each bun. Drizzle with blue cheese dressing, top with arugula, and close sandwiches. Makes 3 mini sandwiches

S
T

For a Southwest flair, top each slider with cheddar cheese and a dollop of refried beans and guacamole.

Sloppy Joe

The everyman's sandwich

Easy to make, economical, and satisfying, Sloppy Joes were the ideal belly-filler during the Great Depression and World War II. As early as the 1890s, American cookbooks listed recipes for hamburger cooked with peppers, onions, tomatoes, and Worcestershire sauce. By the 1930s, this combination had evolved into a classic American sandwich: ground beef, peppers, and onions cooked in a sweet and spicy tomato sauce, served hot—open-faced or closed—on a soft untoasted hamburger bun.

So who named it Sloppy Joe? No one knows for sure, but most historians concur that it evolved from the popular **Loose Meat Sandwich** invented in 1926 by Floyd Angell, founder of Maid-Rite restaurants. Some credit a cook named Joe, whereas others think it's a whole lot simpler: They say "sloppy" refers to the sandwich's distinguishing messiness, and "Joe" is a common all-American name for a common all-American sandwich. One thing most everyone shares is a love for this unpretentious, deliciously gloppy food.

Assemble sandwiches only when you're ready to eat them—wait 10 minutes and you'll be eating a Soggy Joe instead. Skip the silverware—just plop a stack of napkins in the center of the table or, better yet, a roll of paper towels. You'll need them.

2 tablespoons olive oil
1 cup finely chopped yellow onion
½ cup finely diced celery
½ cup finely chopped green pepper
1½ pounds ground beef
1½ to 2 cups tomato sauce (depending on desired sloppiness)
½ cup ketchup
¼ cup light brown sugar
2 tablespoons Worcestershire sauce
2 teaspoons Tabasco
1½ tablespoons red wine vinegar
6 hamburger buns or kaiser rolls

❶ Warm olive oil in a large pan over medium heat. Add onions, celery, and peppers and sauté 2 to 3 minutes, or until just tender. Add beef, stirring to break it up. Cook 10 to 12 minutes or until browned. Drain off excess fat.

❷ Add remaining ingredients (except buns) and simmer uncovered 15 to 20 minutes, or until mixture is thick and a little sloppy but not too soupy. Spoon onto buns and eat immediately. Makes 6

Spaghetti Sandwich

Quick, cheap, and easy

No one knows for sure who created the Spaghetti Sandwich, but everyone agrees that this is one magnificent carb bomb. It is almost always made from reheated leftover spaghetti and usually consumed at home when hungry, alone, and/or short on cash. Although it may seem strange, this sandwich is especially popular in Japan, where it is typically served on a hoagie-style bun and sometimes topped with corn kernels. There are no rules when it comes to making one—just follow your instincts.

---

1 (6-inch) hoagie roll or garlic bread roll
½ cup reheated leftover spaghetti, with sauce
1 to 2 tablespoons warm tomato sauce
A sprinkle of grated Parmesan cheese

Open roll. Add spaghetti. Top with tomato sauce and cheese. If desired, pop under broiler 1 to 2 minutes to lightly toast. Eat immediately.
Makes 1

Sliced bread is not recommended because the spaghetti slides out when you bite into the sandwich. Try adding meatballs or sausage (or both) or a good melting cheese, such as mozzarella or provolone.

Spamwich

Suspicious, yet delicious

Spam has a checkered history in the mainland United States. In 1926, when Jay C. Hormel was looking for a way to use thousands of pounds of pork shoulder leftover at his father's food company, he created a new canned-meat product called Hormel Spiced Ham. Because it did not require refrigeration and was easily transportable, Spam (as it came to be called) was a staple for soldiers during World War II. Considered by many civilians to be a cheap and unappealing meal, the characteristically pink, gelatinous precooked meat has long been reviled; it's been the butt of countless jokes and comic skits, including, most famously, Monty Python's eponymous sketch. The product does, however, have its admirers, especially in Hawaii and much of Asia. Hawaiians are the leading consumers, with every resident averaging 6 cans per year. In fact, Spam is so popular there, it has even appeared on the menus of the islands' McDonald's and Burger King restaurants.

1 tablespoon canola oil

1 (12-ounce) can Hormel Spam,
   cut into 8 slices

4 hamburger buns, split and toasted

1 (8-ounce) can pineapple rings, drained

4 slices American cheese

❶ Warm oil in a large skillet over medium-high heat. Arrange sliced Spam in pan so that pieces do not touch; cook 2 to 3 minutes, flip, and cook an additional 2 to 3 minutes, or until golden brown.

❷ Place 2 slices Spam on each hamburger bun. Top with pineapple rings and cheese. Close sandwiches. Makes 4

S
T

Spam, Spam, Spam!

- **Green Eggs and Spam Sandwich:** Soak peeled, hard-boiled eggs in water mixed with lots of green food coloring, preferably overnight. Drain and slice eggs; then layer them with Spam on sandwich to create this cute, edible tribute to Dr. Seuss.
- **Hot Hawaiian Spamwich:** Assemble sandwich without the pineapple slice. Broil sandwich 3 to 5 minutes or until cheese melts; add pineapple slice and eat while hot.

- **Midwestern Spamwich:** The mainland U.S. Spam sandwich typically consists of two slices of white bread filled with a creamy, saladlike mixture of minced Spam, mayonnaise, relish, spicy mustard, and diced hard-boiled eggs.
- **Spam Monte Cristo:** Place 1 thick slice of Spam with Muenster cheese between 2 pieces of white bread. Dip sandwich in egg beaten with milk, fry in butter, and enjoy the fatty, artificial goodness.

The variations are endless, but most
Spam lovers agree that it tastes best when
sliced and fried until brown and crispy.

Spiedie

The sandwich for skewered food

Spiedini is the Italian word for a skewer of chunks of meat, seafood, cheese, or vegetables that is grilled over a flame or cooked under a broiler. A spiedie is essentially a spiedini served inside a soft submarine roll and typically drizzled with a special sauce or marinade.

The Spiedie is the signature sandwich of Binghamton, New York, where it was introduced by Italian immigrants sometime in the 1920s. Though disputed, its creator is most likely Augustine Iacovelli, an immigrant from Abruzzi, Italy, who began selling the sandwiches in 1939, upon opening his first restaurant, Augies's, in Endicott, New York. Some seventy years later, Binghamton's spiedie pride is unwavering: Each summer approximately 100,000 people attend the city's annual Spiedie Fest and Balloon Rally, which features a contest for the year's best spiedie. Most agree that the yummiest are offered at Lupo's Spiedies. In 1951 the Lupo family opened a corner meat market, where they sold so many spiedies they opened a restaurant in 1978. According to owner Steve Lupo, if you can't make it to Binghamton, try these tips for making an authentic one at home: "Use the best ingredients you can find. Always marinate the meat overnight to make it really tender and delicious. And grill the meat until nicely charred. You don't want to rush it."

You may want to reserve a little of the fresh marinade to drizzle on the finished sandwiches. Or make your own spiedie sauce with olive oil, vinegar, and Italian spices.

S
T

Spiedie

ST

GARLIC-ROSEMARY MARINADE

2 tablespoons olive oil

1 tablespoon balsamic vinegar

Salt and freshly ground black pepper, to taste

2 sprigs fresh or 1 tablespoon dried rosemary

1 garlic clove, thinly sliced

PORK SKEWERS

1½ pounds pork tenderloin, cut into 1½-inch cubes

1 large red bell pepper, cut into 1½-inch pieces

1 large green bell pepper, cut into 1½-inch pieces

1 large sweet onion, cut into 1½-inch pieces

4 (6-inch) submarine rolls

Optional garnishes: fresh lettuce and tomatoes, or sautéed mushrooms

❶ In a small bowl, whisk together oil, vinegar, salt, pepper, rosemary, and garlic. Place meat in a large zip-top plastic bag and pour in marinade. Seal bag and gently shake until meat is thoroughly coated. Chill at least 4 hours or preferably overnight, turning several times.

❷ Soak 4 wooden skewers in water about 1 hour to ensure they won't burn. Preheat grill to medium. Remove pork from refrigerator about 15 minutes before cooking. Thread meat onto skewers, alternating with pepper and onion pieces, so that skewers have equal numbers of meat and vegetable pieces.

❸ Place skewers on grill and cook 4 to 6 minutes, turning as needed, until mildly charred and cooked through. Warm rolls for 1 minute on grill rack. To assemble, place skewer inside a roll; squeeze tightly with one hand and pull out skewer with the other, leaving meat inside the roll. Eat plain, add garnishes, or drizzle with fresh marinade or your favorite spiedie sauce. Serve immediately with fries or onion rings and cold beer. Makes 4

S
T

Quick and Easy Variations

- Spiedie Pockets: To make the Italian American cousin of the **Kofta Pocket** (page 156), stuff grilled meat into halved, warmed pita pockets.

- Delicious substitutes for the pork include boneless leg of lamb and chicken.

Steak and Onion Sandwich

Seriously satisfying

At its most basic, a Steak and Onion Sandwich consists of grilled, broiled, or sautéed flank steak smothered in caramelized onions and served on bread. Other popular toppings include buttery sautéed mushrooms, Swiss or Gruyère cheese, sliced tomato, and sharp greens such as watercress. For a spicier version, season steak and onions with horseradish sauce.

Though Pat Oliveri (founder of Pat's King of Steaks—the iconic **Philly Cheesesteak** eatery) is often credited with creating the first steak sandwich in 1930, Louis Lassen beat him to it. Lassen sold America's first steak sandwiches to hungry local factory workers at Louis' Lunch, the New Haven, Connecticut, sandwich shop he opened in 1895. Word quickly spread, and within a couple decades steak sandwiches were being served at luncheonettes, food trucks, and diners all along the East Coast.

A steak bomb sandwich is a New England specialty. This hot grinder consists of sliced grilled steak and salami that is covered in melted provolone cheese, grilled onions, and sautéed bell peppers and mushrooms.

Steak and Onion Sandwich

½ pound flank steak

¼ teaspoon salt

¼ teaspoon freshly ground black pepper

2 teaspoons canola oil

2 tablespoons butter, divided

1 small yellow onion, thinly sliced

½ teaspoon sugar

1 cup sliced cremini or white button
  mushrooms

½ large green bell pepper, thinly sliced

2 tablespoons Worcestershire sauce

2 torpedo rolls, split down the center

4 slices sharp provolone cheese

❶ Season steak with salt and black pepper. Warm oil in a large skillet over medium heat, add steak, and cook to desired doneness, about 2 minutes per side for medium-rare and 5 minutes per side for medium-well. Transfer steak to a work surface; cover and let stand 5 minutes.

❷ Melt 1 tablespoon of the butter in a separate large skillet over medium-low heat, add onions, and sprinkle with sugar; cook until lightly browned, about 5 minutes. Add mushrooms and peppers; cook 2 to 3 minutes, or until a few brown spots appear. Add Worcestershire sauce and cook another 2 to 3 minutes. Remove from heat.

❸ Butter interior of rolls with remaining 1 tablespoon of butter. Place facedown on a large skillet over medium heat and brown until crispy. Meanwhile, slice cooked steak on the diagonal. Lay 2 cheese slices onto an opened torpedo roll. Top cheese with half the steak, then with half the vegetables. Repeat for the second sandwich. Eat while it's hot. Makes 2

You Say Chivito, I Say Steak Sandwich

- Chacarero: Top steak with tomatoes, green beans, Muenster cheese, and chili peppers to make this Chilean steak sandwich. Pork or chicken are common variations.

- Chivito: To make the sandwich that's been called the national dish of Uruguay, thinly slice filet mignon and wedge it in a long or round roll with ham, bacon, eggs, mozzarella cheese, and vegetables.

S
T

Submarine Sandwich

A hearty loaf filled with cold cuts, cheese, lettuce, tomato, and onions

The Submarine Sandwich originated during the late nineteenth to mid-twentieth century in Italian American communities clustered throughout the northeastern United States. The exact origin is disputed, but most people believe it got its name because the tubular roll made it look like a World War II military submarine. That makes sense if you consider that Groton, Connecticut—which considers itself the sub's birthplace—was home to an active submarine base during World War II, when the sandwiches were served by the thousands to soldiers. The problem is that the term *submarine sandwich* was being used well before the 1940s. In 1910 Dominic Conti, an Italian immigrant, opened a grocery store in New Jersey where he sold large meat-and-cheese-filled sandwiches that were based on a recipe from Italy. Supposedly in 1927 he saw the recovered 1878 submarine *Holland I* and said, "It looks like the sandwich I sell at my store." From then on, the sandwich was called a submarine, later shortened to sub. No matter who coined the name, Americans love their subs, thanks in part to the Subway sandwich-shop chain, founded in 1965.

Various regional terms include blimpie (Hoboken, New Jersey, which is home to the Blimpie sandwich chain); bomber (Buffalo, New York); **Grinder** (most of New England, except Boston); **Hero** (New York City); **Hoagie** (Philadelphia); Italian sandwich (Maine); spuckie (Boston); torpedo (New Jersey, New York, San Diego, and others); wedge (parts of Westchester County, New York, the Bronx, and upstate New York); and zeppelin or zep (Norristown, Pennsylvania, and parts of New Jersey). Simply adjust amounts and types of cold cuts and cheese to easily turn this sandwich into any number of subs, such as ham and cheese, turkey and Swiss, or roast beef.

S
T

1 (6-inch) roll, sliced lengthwise

2 teaspoons mayonnaise

2 teaspoons yellow mustard

¼ cup shredded romaine or iceberg lettuce

3 thick slices tomato

4 thin slices red onion

2 thin slices turkey

2 thin slices boiled ham

2 thin slices American cheese

6 slices sweet pickle

❶ Place sliced roll on a cutting board. Spread mayo and mustard on each half.

❷ On the bottom piece of bread, layer lettuce, tomato, onions, turkey, ham, cheese, and pickles. Close sandwich. Makes 1

The submarine was not the first undersea vessel ever developed. Among its predecessors were several colorfully dubbed prototypes: the Turtle, the Alligator, *le Diable Marin* ("the Sea Devil"), and the Intelligent Whale. But who wants to eat a sea devil sandwich?

S
T

Submarine Sandwich

Tea Sandwiches

Fancy little teatime snacks

Dainty sandwiches made of thinly sliced and buttered crustless white bread and various light fillings, such as cucumber, jam, egg salad, and smoked salmon, earned the name "tea sandwiches" because they were first served with afternoon tea in the United Kingdom. They were a mark of one's wealth during Victorian and Edwardian times: Only the affluent could afford a light meal to keep them satisfied before their more substantial evening repast. Though most commonly served as part of a tea service, these light bites are currently enjoyed as an anytime snack in Britain. Elsewhere, they are typically found at formal teas and ladies' luncheons.

These classic examples are made of two thin slices of buttered, crustless white bread topped with vinegar-marinated sliced cucumbers sprinkled with salt and black pepper. To avoid soggy sandwiches, eat them soon after assembling. Or, prior to assembly, sprinkle the cucumber slices with salt and let drain 1 to 2 hours, then pat dry with a paper towel. For variety, try chive butter or mayonnaise instead of plain butter; sprinkle cucumber with lemon juice and extra-virgin olive oil; or serve with a layer of avocado slices, alfalfa sprouts, or smoked salmon.

¼ large seedless cucumber, peeled
    and thinly sliced
2 tablespoons white wine vinegar
8 slices white bread
4 tablespoons softened butter
Salt and freshly ground black pepper
¼ cup watercress

❶ In a bowl, cover sliced cucumber with vinegar; marinate 30 to 45 minutes; drain. Place bread on a clean surface and spread a thin layer of butter on each slice.

❷ Layer overlapping cucumber slices on 4 of the bread slices, sprinkle with salt and pepper, and top with watercress. Close sandwiches, press firmly, and cut off crusts; then cut each sandwich into 4 triangles. Makes 4 full, 8 half, or 16 quarter sandwiches

Toasted Chocolate Sandwich

A melty crisp chocolate treat

According to Mark Zanger's *American History Cookbook*, the Toasted Chocolate Sandwich first appeared in a 1938 collection of recipes from a ladies auxiliary group in Idaho. It consisted of nestling several pieces of a Hershey's milk chocolate bar between two crunchy slices of toasted bread. Whether the recipe was from the ladies or from Hershey's is unknown. Although chocolate was enjoyed at first only by the affluent, because of its high price, in 1900 Hershey's introduced affordable milk chocolate bars for the masses. It is surprising that these sandwiches never reached the heights of popularity attained by other American sandwiches, such as the **Peanut Butter and Jelly** and **Fluffernutter**. Today most chocolate sandwiches on the menus of bistros and high-end bakeries are made with a European flair: rich, dark chocolate melted on toasted artisanal bread, drizzled with extra-virgin olive oil, and sprinkled with coarse sea salt.

2 slices crusty French bread

1 teaspoon extra-virgin olive oil

2 ounces of your favorite dark chocolate, preferably 60%–70% cacao, cut into squares

A couple pinches coarse sea salt

❶ Preheat broiler. Place both slices of bread on a baking sheet and broil until lightly toasted, 30 to 60 seconds. Turn slices over; drizzle with olive oil and cover with chocolate squares.

❷ Broil just until bread is golden and chocolate begins to melt, 30 to 60 seconds (avoid melting the chocolate completely). Remove from oven; sprinkle with salt, and smile. It's time to eat. Makes 1

When In Doubt, Add Nutella

- Peanut Butter and Chocolate Sandwich: Omit the olive oil and salt. Spread 1 tablespoon of your favorite peanut butter on bread; use either dark or milk chocolate. Feel free to add sliced bananas.

- Chocolate and Raspberry Panini: Use dark chocolate and 1 to 2 tablespoons raspberry marmalade. Make the sandwich in a panini press.

S
T

Toasted Chocolate Sandwich

Tomato Sandwich

Tomato Sandwich

A simple summertime snack

Often referred to as a summer tomato sandwich, this is simplicity itself: two slices of white bread slathered with mayonnaise and topped with slices of the sweetest, juiciest vine-ripened beefsteak tomato available. A sprinkling of salt and pepper is the only adornment this sandwich needs. For many the simple Tomato Sandwich is a highlight of summertime since that's the only time of year when vine-ripened beefsteaks are available. Though eaten throughout North America, these sandwiches are especially popular in the southern United States, where they are affectionately called 'mater sandwiches.

For a first-rate experience, use only fresh, ripe beefsteak tomatoes that have never been refrigerated. For extra tang, whisk some fresh lemon zest and juice into the mayonnaise. Try topping tomato slices with thinly sliced Vidalia onions. Butter and toast the bread if you like. For a heartier sandwich, try a denser multigrain or whole wheat bread. Serve this juicy summertime classic with a glass of cold iced tea—and a lot of napkins.

---

1 tablespoon mayonnaise
2 slices white bread
½ beefsteak tomato, thinly sliced
Salt and freshly ground black pepper

Spread mayonnaise on both bread slices. Top with tomato slices and sprinkle with salt and black pepper. Close the sandwich and eat immediately. Makes 1

S
T

To prevent soggy bread, either eat this sandwich immediately after assembling or toast the bread first. Just don't drain the tomatoes—it's no fun eating a tomato sandwich unless the succulent juice drips down your chin as you chew.

Torta

Inexpensive, fast, and filling

A *torta* is a popular Mexican sandwich consisting of a split *telera*—a flat, mildly crusty white roll—packed with any of various meat or vegetarian fillings, ranging from chorizo and chicken to flank steak and scrambled eggs. Common garnishes include avocado, refried beans, hot sauce, lettuce, and tomato.

It has been called Mexico's version of the **Hoagie**, a Mexican **Hamburger**, and a taco on bread. In fact, it's none of those. It's a Torta, the beloved national sandwich of Mexico that has numerous regional incarnations. Tortas are consummate street food—inexpensive, fast, and filling—so don't go searching for them at posh eateries. In the United States, and especially in Houston, Texas, you'll likely find them served from Mexican food trucks and taquerias.

Telera rolls are available at Mexican specialty markets, but a soft crusted baguette is a good substitute. Mexican *crema* is a sour cream available in the refrigerated section of Mexican specialty markets as well as many major supermarkets; regular sour cream is a good substitute.

---

1 teaspoon canola oil
½ small red onion, thinly sliced
¼ pound chorizo, sliced on the diagonal
2 eggs
¼ teaspoon salt
¼ teaspoon freshly ground black pepper
1 to 2 teaspoons hot sauce
1 tablespoon crema
1 telera roll, split in half and lightly toasted
2 tablespoons refried beans
2 slices ripe avocado or 1 tablespoon
  prepared guacamole

❶ Warm oil in a large skillet over medium heat. Add onions and chorizo and sauté about 5 minutes, or until meat is browned and crisp. In a small bowl, whisk eggs, salt, pepper, and hot sauce. Add to skillet; stir frequently until eggs are cooked through yet still soft.

❷ Spread crema on both halves of the roll. On the bottom half, add refried beans; top with chorizo-egg mixture and avocado. Serve immediately. Makes 1

This breakfast torta pairs well with a glass of freshly squeezed orange juice and a big mug of strong coffee.

Torta

Tuna Niçoise Sandwich

S
T

Tuna Niçoise Sandwich

Salade Niçoise on bread

Commonly known in France and around the world as a *pan bagnat*, this sandwich is a cosmopolitan version of the **Tuna Salad Sandwich**. It is traditionally made with a round, white, crusty roll that is generously filled with a mixture of olive-oil-packed tuna, anchovies, olives, capers, and hard-boiled eggs; think of it as a *salade Niçoise* served on bread.

The pan bagnat is a beloved specialty of Nice, where it can be found anywhere from street-side cafes to beach blanket picnics. Its name means "bathed" or "wet bread," referring to the oil-and-vinegar dressing that seeps deliciously into the bread's interior. When making a pan bagnat, use the highest quality ingredients available, especially for the olive-oil-packed tuna, kalamata olives, and bread. For best results, make the sandwich a day ahead, wrap tightly in plastic wrap, and place in the refrigerator with a heavy dish or pan resting on top so that the juices can soak into the bread.

This is a case where the right bread is critical: If it isn't crusty enough, the liquid will make it soggy. The French typically use a round white loaf with a crusty exterior and somewhat soft interior that is difficult to find in markets or bakeries outside France. Kaiser rolls are a good substitute, but most people use a crusty French baguette. Some of the bread may be scooped out to accommodate the fillings.

S
T

DRESSING

2 teaspoons extra-virgin olive oil

1 tablespoon red wine vinegar

1 teaspoon lemon juice

½ garlic clove, minced

⅛ teaspoon salt

⅛ teaspoon freshly ground black pepper

OLIVE-ANCHOVY SPREAD

2 teaspoons capers, drained and coarsely
    chopped

¼ cup kalamata olives, coarsely chopped

6 anchovy fillets, drained and coarsely
    chopped, or 1 teaspoon anchovy paste

2 tablespoons chopped fresh parsley

1 (12-inch) French baguette, halved lengthwise

6 ounces canned tuna in olive oil, drained and
    flaked into chunks with a fork

¼ cup thinly sliced red onion

4 thin slices tomato

1 hard-boiled egg, cooled and thinly sliced

❶ In a small bowl, whisk together dressing
ingredients; set aside. In a separate small bowl,
combine capers, olives, anchovies, and parsley;
mash with a fork until a coarse paste forms,
then set aside.

❷ If desired, scoop out a bit of the bread.
Brush inside with dressing and spread olive-
anchovy spread evenly over bread.

❸ Add tuna and top with slices of red onion,
tomato, and hard-boiled egg. Close sandwich
and press firmly. Eat at room temperature.
Makes 1 big enough to share

S
T

Tuna Salad Sandwich

Humble gourmet

This sandwich typically consists of canned chunk light or white albacore tuna mixed with mayonnaise, celery, and onions and heaped onto toasted white bread. There are, however, numerous variations. Some are served as subs in long torpedo rolls and topped with pickles, lettuce, and tomato; others have more sophisticated add-ins like black olives, capers, or sun-dried tomatoes. Gourmet tuna salad sandwiches are often made with artisanal bread and more expensive olive-oil packed Italian or Spanish tuna.

Since it was imported from France and Italy and considered a delicacy, canned tuna was not widely consumed in mid- to late-nineteenth-century America. Once tuna canneries opened in the late nineteenth and early twentieth centuries, prices fell and consumption went up. Canned tuna was considered a healthy, relatively low-cost meal. With the introduction of sliced soft white bread in the 1930s, tuna salad sandwiches became a popular brown bag lunch, which they still are today.

This recipe merely flakes the tuna into chunks; if you prefer your tuna salad as a spread, use ⅓ cup mayonnaise and mash the tuna with a fork until it forms a spreadable paste.

S
T

1 (6-ounce) can chunk light or chunk white tuna, drained and flaked with a fork

½ cup finely chopped celery, including some leaves

2 tablespoons finely chopped scallion or chives

⅓ to ½ cup mayonnaise

1½ teaspoons Dijon mustard

2 tablespoons sweet relish

2 teaspoons fresh lemon juice

¼ teaspoon salt

¼ teaspoon freshly ground black pepper

2 tablespoons softened butter

4 thick slices white or whole wheat bread

4 thin slices tomato

4 leaves lettuce, such as romaine, iceberg, or green or red leaf

❶ In a small bowl, mix together tuna, celery, scallions or chives, mayonnaise, mustard, relish, lemon juice, salt, and pepper.

❷ Butter bread, and toast until golden brown. Top 2 pieces with tomato, lettuce, and tuna salad. Close sandwiches, cut in half on the diagonal, and serve immediately. Makes 2

A Foot-Long Tuna Salad

- Tuna Salad Sub: Tuck tuna salad into 2 (6-inch) Italian rolls or French baguettes split down the middle and lightly toasted with butter or olive oil. Garnish with your choice of sliced tomato, lettuce, pickles, sliced Swiss or American cheese, or crispy cooked bacon.

S
T

Simple Tuna Salad

Like a good pair of dark-wash jeans, a classic tuna salad never goes out of style. This traditional recipe is perfect for making tuna melts, a hybrid variation of the **Tuna Salad Sandwich** and the **Crab Melt** that's typically served open-faced on rye bread and topped with tomato slices and American or cheddar cheese. The whole shebang is then placed under a broiler 3 or 4 minutes, or until melted and toasty.

1 (5- to 6-ounce) can solid white tuna
   in water, drained

2 tablespoons mayonnaise

2 tablespoons finely chopped celery, optional

2 tablespoons finely chopped yellow onion,
   optional

⅛ teaspoon salt

⅛ teaspoon black pepper

In a small bowl combine all ingredients. Use a fork to break tuna into small pieces. Mix to combine. Makes enough for 2 sandwiches

S
T

Turkey Sandwich
Gobble, gobble

Thinly sliced white turkey meat sandwiched between two slices of bread, most commonly garnished with mayonnaise or mustard, lettuce, and tomato, makes a classic Turkey Sandwich. Other popular toppings include sliced Swiss cheese, sliced avocado, sprouts, and cranberry sauce.

According to the National Turkey Federation, as of 2007, the average American consumes 17.5 pounds of turkey per year. In 1970 nearly 50% of the turkey consumed in the United States was served during holiday dinners; today that figure is only about 30%. That means Americans are eating a lot of Turkey Sandwiches year-round. It's no wonder: Turkey has been successfully marketed as the low-calorie, healthy alternative to beef and pork.

---

2 tablespoons prepared maple-flavored barbecue sauce

2 slices whole wheat or multigrain bread

2 slices turkey breast

1 slice smoked Gouda

4 thin slices sweet onion

Spread barbecue sauce on one side of each bread slice. On one slice, barbecue-sauce side up, layer turkey, cheese, and onions. Top with second slice, barbecue-sauce side down. Makes 1

From Brown Bag Lunch to Gourmet Snack

- Turkey with basil pesto and sliced mozzarella on crusty Italian bread.
- Turkey with hummus and roasted red peppers in a pita pocket.
- Turkey with pickles on a sub roll.
- Turkey with Brie and apricot jelly on multigrain bread.
- Turkey with cream cheese, cranberry sauce, and sliced onions on French country bread.

S
T

Veal and Pepper Sandwich

Tender veal on crusty bread

A Veal and Pepper Sandwich consists of veal that is simmered until tender in a sauce of tomatoes, wine, and herbs. It is served on sturdy, crusty bread that can absorb the sauce while maintaining its shape. Like the **Sausage and Pepper Sandwich**, veal and peppers is a Neapolitan specialty that was introduced to America by Italian immigrants at the turn of the twentieth century. Unlike sausage and peppers, however, veal and peppers is made more like a stew. It's a bit more labor intensive, but wholly worth the effort.

Toast me, baby! Top this sandwich with sliced mozzarella or sharp provolone and broil 2 minutes, or until the cheese melts and the bread is toasty and golden. Serve with a bottle of your favorite red wine and an antipasto salad for a classic casual Italian dinner.

U
V

1¼ pounds boneless veal shoulder or "stew" veal, cut into 1-inch medallions

⅛ teaspoon salt

⅛ teaspoon freshly ground black pepper

¼ cup all-purpose flour

¼ cup olive oil, divided

1 medium yellow onion, thinly sliced

1 small green bell pepper, cut into thin strips

1 small red bell pepper, cut into thin strips

1 cup thinly sliced cremini or white button mushrooms

⅓ cup red wine

1 (20-ounce) can Italian crushed tomatoes, juices reserved

1 teaspoon dried basil

¼ teaspoon crushed red pepper flakes

6 ciabatta rolls or other crusty Italian rolls, split lengthwise

❶ Season veal with salt and black pepper and dredge in flour until completely coated. Warm 2 tablespoons of the oil in a large skillet over medium heat. Add veal and cook, stirring occasionally, until browned all over, about 10 minutes. Transfer to a warm plate.

❷ In the same skillet, add the remaining 2 tablespoons oil. Add onions, peppers, mushrooms, and salt. Cook, stirring occasionally, until vegetables are lightly browned and tender, about 8 to 10 minutes. Transfer to a bowl and set aside.

❸ In the same skillet, add red wine and simmer 1 minute. Add tomatoes and their juices, basil, and red pepper flakes. Return cooked veal to skillet. Bring sauce to a low boil; as soon as it starts to bubble, reduce heat to low. Partially cover and simmer 35 to 40 minutes, or until veal is completely tender; if sauce reduces too much, add a little water or red wine. Return cooked vegetables to skillet and heat through, about 3 minutes. Season to taste with salt and pepper.

❹ Scoop veal and peppers into rolls. Spoon as much extra sauce on top as you like. Eat immediately. Makes 6

U
V

Veal Parmesan Sub

Fried cutlets smothered with red sauce and melted mozzarella

Several centuries ago, a breaded veal dish from Parma, Italy, that was *not* served with tomatoes or cheese was called *Parmigiana*, in honor of the region. Over time, various regional culinary influences—namely the addition of tomatoes and mozzarella—transformed the dish into something completely different. The name, however, remained the same. The veal (and chicken) parmesan sandwiches that we eat today were introduced by Italian immigrants and are considered classic Italian American cuisine. The Veal Parmesan Sub, also known by various regional names, such as **Hero**, **Grinder**, or **Hoagie**, is a staple on the menus of Italian delis and pizza parlors throughout the United States.

If desired, top veal with sliced provolone or mozzarella cheese and place sandwiches under the broiler until cheese melts. When serving for dinner, pair with a mesclun salad, a glass of red wine, and some Frank Sinatra crooning in the background.

Making veal parmesan from scratch is well worth the effort. Consider making a double batch to use for leftovers. Stored in an airtight container in the refrigerator, it will last 4 to 5 days.

U
V

Veal Parmesan Sub

U
V

2 eggs
2 tablespoons milk
⅛ teaspoon crushed red pepper flakes
⅛ teaspoon salt
¼ cup all-purpose flour
⅔ cup plain bread crumbs
3 tablespoons olive oil
1 pound veal cutlets (about ½ inch thick)
1 (28- to 32-ounce) jar tomato sauce
¼ cup grated Parmigiano Reggiano cheese
¾ cup shredded mozzarella
4 to 6 (6-inch-long) Italian or torpedo rolls,
    split lengthwise and toasted

❶ Prehead oven to 375°F. In a wide, shallow bowl, whisk eggs, milk, red pepper, and salt. Place flour in a second wide, shallow bowl, and bread crumbs in a third.

❷ Place oil in a large skillet over medium heat. Dip one veal cutlet at a time in flour, then in egg mixture, allowing excess to drip into the bowl. Dredge in bread crumbs, ensuring that entire cutlet is evenly coated. Cook in skillet 2 to 3 minutes on each side until golden brown and crisp. Place on a paper-towel-lined dish. Repeat with remaining veal.

❸ Cover the bottom of a 9-inch round or 8-inch square baking dish with a layer of tomato sauce. Add a layer of veal (larger pieces on the bottom), then a layer of both cheeses. Repeat until all ingredients are used.

❹ Bake 25 to 30 minutes, or until sauce begins to bubble and cheese turns golden brown. Let cool 5 minutes before slicing cutlets into strips. Fill each roll with several strips of veal and serve hot. Makes 4 to 6

Homemade tomato sauce makes a good sandwich even better.
For recipes, see pages 85 and 168.

U
V

Veggie Sandwich

A deliciously skinny sandwich

A very distant cousin of such meaty sandwiches as the **Italian Beef** and the **Philly Cheesesteak**, the Veggie Sandwich consists of fresh, healthy fillings, like cucumbers, radishes, sprouts, and hummus, packed neatly between two slices of multigrain bread.

Vegetarianism has deep roots: In late-seventeenth-century Europe some people chose a fleshless diet for moral reasons as well as practical ones (since meatless diets were less expensive). Over time vegetarianism spread to the West and gained influential followers among physicians, authors, and church leaders; it reached its heyday in the 1960s and '70s, when it became associated with the counterculture. Today vegetarianism is much more mainstream, with many cities boasting meat-free restaurants and traditional eateries offering vegetarian fare, from veggie burgers (page 127) to mock-chicken sandwiches to tempeh **Reubens**.

---

2 to 3 tablespoons hummus
2 slices multigrain bread
4 thin slices cucumber
4 thin slices tomato
1 radish, thinly sliced
1 to 2 tablespoons fresh sprouts

❶ Spread hummus on one side of both slices of bread.

❷ Layer veggies, starting with cucumbers and ending with sprouts, on 1 slice of bread. Top with second slice and close sandwich. Makes 1

Veggie sandwiches are ideal for picnics: They can be made ahead, are easily transportable, and can withstand warm weather. Serve with a side of veggie chips or potato salad and some cold lemonade.

Walleye Sandwich
No ordinary Filet-O-Fish

This classic **Fish Sandwich** is a cracker-coated, fried walleye fillet served on either a kaiser or a hoagie-style roll and topped with shredded lettuce, tomato, and tartar sauce.

Named for its large, milky eyes, the walleye has been Minnesota's official state fish since 1965; and if Minnesota had an official state sandwich, there is little doubt it would be this one. In fact, it's difficult *not* to find a Walleye Sandwich on the menus of most Minnesota restaurants and bars.

Walleye is difficult to find outside the northern United States and Canada, but it's available online. Good substitutes include mild-flavored white fish such as flounder, haddock, and sole.

Serve with a side of crunchy onion rings
or French fries, some lemon wedges, and
an icy cold bottle of beer.

W
X
Y
Z

FRIED WALLEYE FILLETS

¼ cup all-purpose flour

1 egg, lightly beaten

¼ cup whole milk

½ cup crushed saltines

¼ teaspoon salt

¼ teaspoon black pepper

4 (4-ounce) walleye fillets, patted dry
with a paper towel

⅓ to ½ cup canola oil

½ cup bottled tartar sauce

4 hoagie-style or kaiser rolls,
toasted or untoasted

8 thin slices tomato

½ cup shredded lettuce

12 pickle chips, optional

❶ Put flour in a wide, shallow dish. In another, lightly whisk egg and milk, and in a third mix saltines, salt, and pepper. Dredge each piece of fish in flour, dip in egg mixture (allowing excess to drip into dish), and dredge in saltines.

❷ Pour oil into a wide skillet to a depth of ½ to 1 inch. Warm over medium heat to 350°F. (Use a deep-fry thermometer or test by dropping a little batter into the oil; it should rise quickly to the surface and be surrounded by tiny bubbles.) Using tongs, gently put fish fillets in hot oil one at a time and cook 5 minutes per side, or until golden brown on the outside and flaky on the inside. Place fish on a paper-towel-lined plate, and fry remaining fillets.

❸ Spread tartar sauce on inside of each bun. Place a fish fillet on the bottom half of each. Top each with 2 slices tomato, 2 tablespoons shredded lettuce, and 3 pickle chips (if desired). Close sandwiches and eat immediately. Makes 4

Other Fish to Fry

- BLFT: Add crispy cooked white fish to a traditional BLT.
- BBQ Walleye Sandwich: Substitute your favorite barbecue sauce for tartar sauce.

- Spicy Walleye Sandwich: To turn up the heat, substitute horseradish sauce for tartar sauce and add sliced onions.

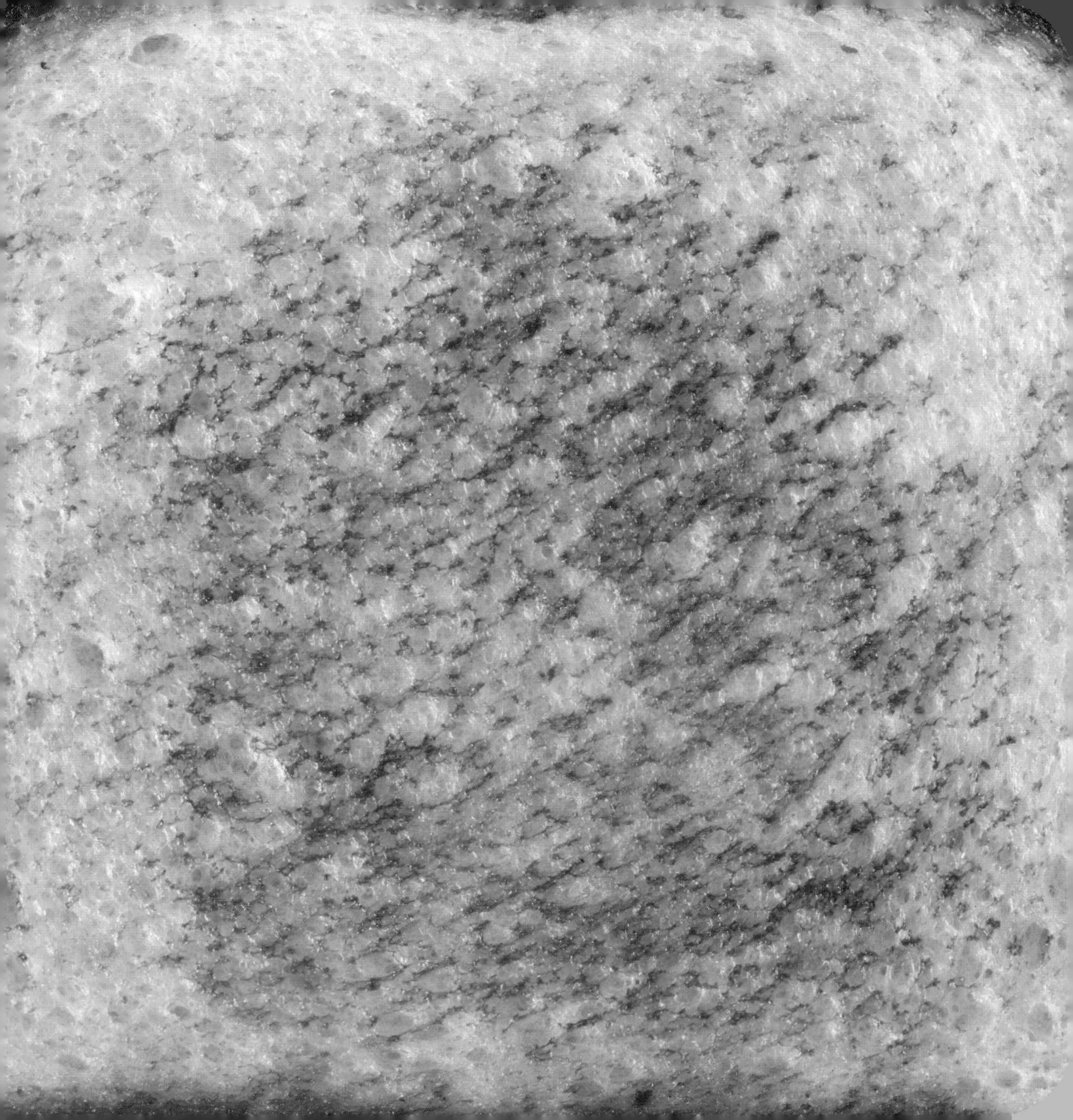

Selected Bibliography

Books for Sandwich Lovers

Beard, James. *James Beard's American Cookery.* New York: Little, Brown, 1972.

Colicchio, Tom. *'Wichcraft: Craft a Sandwich into a Meal—and a Meal into a Sandwich.* New York: Clarkson Potter, 2009.

Davidson, Alan. *The Oxford Companion to Food.* 2d ed. Oxford: Oxford University Press, 2006.

Lindgren, Glenn M., Raúl Musibay, and Jorge Castillo. *Three Guys From Miami Cook Cuban.* Layton, Utah: Gibbs Smith, 2004.

Lukins, Sheila. *U.S.A. Cookbook.* New York: Workman, 1997.

Mariani, John F. *The Encyclopedia of American Food & Drink.* New York: Lebhar-Friedman Books, 1999.

Mercuri, Becky. *American Sandwich: Great Eats from All 50 States.* Layton, Utah: Gibbs Smith, 1994.

Smith, Andrew. *The Oxford Companion to American Food and Drink.* New York: Oxford University Press, 2007.

Stern, Jane, and Michael Stern. *Roadfood Sandwiches: Recipes and Lore from Our Favorite Shops Coast to Coast.* New York: Houghton Mifflin, 2007.

Zanger, Mark. *The American History Cookbook.* Westport, Conn.: Greenwood Press, 2003.

Websites for Sandwich Lovers

Between the Bread
Epicurious
Everybody Likes Sandwiches
Food Timeline
Road Food
Scanwiches
Serious Eats
Unbreaded
What's Cooking America

All-in-One Breakfast
Sandwich, page 3

Banana Split
Sandwich, page 16

Bánh Mì, page 17

Index of Sandwiches

Variations and alternate names appear in italics.

BLT, page 20

Bresaola and Arugula
Sandwich, page 29

Caprese Sandwich,
page 32

Chicken Cutlet
Sandwich, page 33

Chip Butty, page 42

Chow Mein Sandwich,
page 46

Crab Melt, page 54

Curried Chicken Salad
Sandwich, page 66

Dagwood, page 70

The Elvis, page 87

Falafel Pitas, page 90

Fluffernutter, page 95

Greek Salad Pocket, page 110

Hamburger, page 125

Hot Dog, page 139

Ice Cream Sandwich,
page 146

Italian Tuna Salad
Sandwich, page 151

Loose Meat Sandwich,
page 164

Monte Cristo,
page 173

Nutella Sandwich,
page 183

Panini, page 187

Peanut Butter and Jelly,
page 195

Philly Cheesesteak,
page 202

Pound Cake Sandwich,
page 212

Sausage and Pepper
Sandwich, page 234

Sloppy Joe, page 238

Spamwich, page 243

Steak and Onion
Sandwich, page 249

Toasted Chocolate
Sandwich, page 257

Tuna Niçoise
Sandwich, page 264

Veggie Sandwich,
page 278

Walleye Sandwich,
page 281

Metric Conversion Chart

For international sandwich lovers

Volume

U.S.	Metric
¼ tsp	1.25 ml
½ tsp	2.5 ml
1 tsp	5 ml
1 tbsp (3 tsp)	15 ml
1 fl oz (2 tbsp)	30 ml
¼ cup 60 ml	
⅓ cup	80 ml
½ cup	120 ml
1 cup	240 ml
1 pint (2 cups)	480 ml
1 quart (2 pints)	960 ml
1 gallon (4 quarts)	3.84 liters

Weight

U.S.	Metric
1 oz	28 g
4 oz (¼ lb)	113 g
8 oz (½ lb)	227 g
12 oz (¾ lb)	340 g
16 oz (1 lb)	454 g
2.2 lb	1 kg

Length

Inches	Centimeters
¼	0.65
½	1.25
1	2.50
2	5.00
3	7.50
4	10.0
5	12.5
6	15.0
7	17.5
8	20.5
9	23.0
10	25.5
12	30.5
15	38.0

Oven Temperature

Degrees Fahrenheit	Degrees Centigrade	British Gas Marks
200	93	—
250	120	½
275	140	1
300	150	2
325	165	3
350	175	4
375	190	5
400	200	6
450	230	8

About

In search of the perfect sandwich

Author SUSAN RUSSO writes for NPR's Kitchen Window and posts stories, recipes, and photos on her popular food blog, Food Blogga (which is Rhode Island-ese for "food blogger"). She is the coauthor of *Recipes Every Man Should Know* (Quirk, 2010). She resides in San Diego. And she is forever indebted to her Italian mother for teaching her how to make a good meatball sub.

Photographer MATT ARMENDARIZ is a man obsessed with food, drink, and everything in between, as evidenced by his food blog, Matt Bites, and his cookbook dedicated to fair food, party food, and all food served *On a Stick!* He resides in Los Angeles. Let the record show that Matt is a true sandwich champion for trying every single sandwich in this book at least once—and some more times than he'd care to admit.